An **ART WORLD EXPLORER** *guide*

VENICE
CONTEMPORARY ART
2019

BIENNALE GUIDE INCLUDING COLLATERAL EVENTS & 30 INDEPENDENT EXHIBITIONS

The 58th Venice Art Biennale, 'May You Live In Interesting Times', ran from 11 May to 24 November 2019. Coinciding with it were many major independent art shows. This book – which covers over 200 pavilions, exhibitions, and artists – is intended as a handy one-stop resource for anyone who still needs the information, such as researchers, writers, students, artists, gallerists, journalists, art historians, and curators.

BY VICI MACDONALD

Vici MacDonald is a former editor of contemporary art magazine *Art World*, and has contributed design and editorial to periodicals including *The Art Newspaper* and *Tate* magazine. She has art directed specialist publications for major art world events such as Art Basel, Frieze, and Pacific Standard Time. She has also created guides to several previous Venice Biennales.

BIENNALE ARTE
2019

May You
Live In
Interesting
Times

11.05.—24.11.2019
VENEZIA
GIARDINI/ARSENALE

orario / opening hours 10–18
chiuso il lunedì / closed on mondays
www.labiennale.org

 La Biennale di Venezia
 labiennale
 la_Biennale #BiennaleArte2019

swatch

la Biennale di Venezia

Arte
Architettura
Cinema
Danza
Musica
Teatro
Archivio Storico

CONTENTS

INTRODUCTION

A brief introduction to using this guide, and general information about the Venice Biennale.

MAPS

Every exhibition listed in this guide is marked on these maps, making it easy to see at a glance which art shows are near to each other (or wherever you are researching), and also the closest waterbus stops.

MAIN SHOW FLOOR PLANS

Floor plan diagrams for the central exhibition, 'May You Live in Interesting Times', showing the artist placements for 'Proposition A' (Arsenale) and 'Proposition B' (Giardini), plus locations of the Arsenale's national pavilions.

EXHIBITION CHECKLIST

Listed in alphabetical order, all 90 national pavilions and 21 collateral events plus 30 selected exhibitions. Includes addresses, times and descriptions, plus check boxes to tick off those seen, and space to add your own notes.

ARTIST CHECKLIST

Listed in alphabetical order, all 84 individual artists in the main exhibition, 'May You Live in Interesting Times'. Includes biographical info, plus check boxes to tick off those seen, and space to add your own notes. At the end is a jotter spread for further notes, with a reminder list of all the artists included.

NOTEBOOK

A brief section of jotter pages with blank lined and unlined pages, for recording your own words and visuals.

INDEX

All the artists and venues listed in alphabetical order, for quick reference.

A billboard outside the Giardini for the Venice Biennale's 2019 edition, titled 'May You Live in Interesting Times.'

ABOUT THIS GUIDE

If there's one event that the art world venerates above all others, it's the Venice Biennale, inaugurated in 1895 and still going strong. In 2019 this long-running showcase celebrated its 58th edition, titled 'May You Live in Interesting Times'. There was so much art to see during its six-month run, and such fragmentary information available, that it can be difficult to get a handle on it all — hence this guide. It's split into the following sections:

MAPS

The maps show every exhibition listed, plus all the waterbus (vaporetto) stops, so you can easily see what else is nearby. There are full and detail maps of Venice city, plus close-up maps of the Arsenale and Giardini sites. The numbers on the maps cross-refer to the Exhibition Checklist and Venue Index. These give full street addresses, and can be used with an online map to get accurate location info.

MAIN SHOW FLOOR PLANS

These show the layout of 'May You Live in Interesting Times' for 'Proposition A' (Arsenale) and 'Proposition B' (Giardini). A key gives the location of each artist, plus the Arsenale pavilions.

EXHIBITION CHECKLIST

Each of the 101 Biennale presentations, known as National Pavilions (colloquially — the official Biennale term is Participating Countries) and Collateral Events, is listed in alphabetical order, along with 30 highlights from the many general art exhibitions that coincided with the Biennale. You'll find descriptions, addresses, and opening times, plus space to add notes.

ARTIST CHECKLIST

Similarly listed are the 79 artists and groups (a total of 84 individuals in all) in the main themed show, 'May You Live in Interesting Times', which was curated by Ralph Rugoff. With each exhibitor showing works in the two main venues of the Giardini and Arsenale, there was a huge amount of art on offer, so this Artist Checklist is a simple way to keep track.

JOURNAL

Next comes some space for adding personal notes and comments. The left-hand pages are lined for writing in; the right-hand pages are unlined, for sketches and freeform notes.

ARTIST & VENUE INDEX

A quick way to find anything in this book. All the Biennale artists and venues — plus headlining artists from the general exhibitions in this guide — are listed with full details, in alphabetical order.

ABOUT THE BIENNALE

The Venice Biennale has two main venues, the Giardini and the Arsenale. These require a ticket for entry – one ticket gives access to both places. The rest of the official shows are spread throughout Venice city, and are usually free to enter, with no Biennale ticket required.

THE GIARDINI

The permanent national pavilions in the Giardini are what distinguish Venice from other such biennales. Developed from 1907 onwards, these buildings offer a fascinating collage of architectural styles, from Hungary's ornate mosaics to Switzerland's refined modernism. They also reflect the tides of geopolitics, with some bearing now-defunct names such as Yugoslavia.

THE ARSENALE

This ancient military site takes up a sixth of Venice's total area, and is usually closed to the public – but during the Biennale, its magnificent grounds are open to all. There's much to explore, including the famous Corderie (an immensely long ex-ropemaking works), the arcaded shipyards of Gaggiandre, acres of brick warehouses, and a historic 19th-century crane. Photo opportunities abound, and its peaceful backwaters feel a world away from the general Venetian frenzy.

VENICE CITY

Many Biennale shows spill out into Venice city itself, occupying a host of fascinating buildings, such as grand palazzi, places of worship, municipal buildings, and defunct shops. Visiting such venues is an experience in itself, and takes you to parts of the island that most tourists never reach.

DATES & TIMES

11 May-24 November 2019
(Some shows ended slightly earlier than planned due to the catastrophic November floods)
Closed on Mondays (except 13 May, 2 September, 18 November)
Giardini & Arsenale: open 10:00 to 18:00 (10am to 6pm)
Arsenale: on Fridays and Saturdays, until 5 October, open 10:00 to 20:00 (10am to 8pm)

TICKETS

Every Biennale has various ticket deals available, and if staying for several days, consider one that allows multiple entry. You can then freely come and go between Venice city and the Arsenale and Giardini, which given their vastness, can be a relief – and allows popping out for lunch. Tickets can be bought online, and are also easy to buy at the gates (but note that there's often a lengthy queue). See the Biennale's website for full details – the 2019 address is below.

www.labiennale.org/en/art/2019

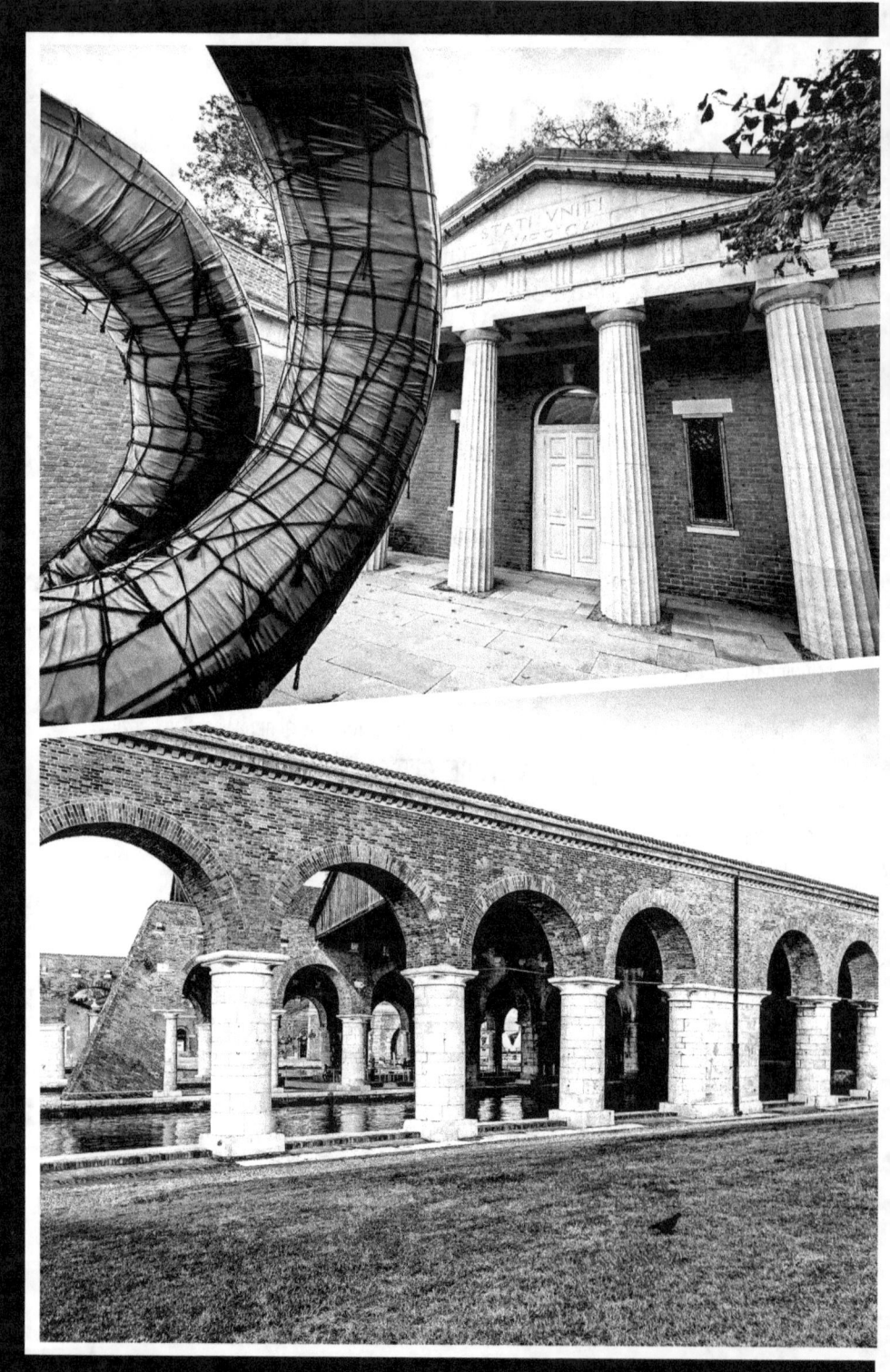

MAPS

FOR THE 2019 / 58ᵀᴴ VENICE ART BIENNALE

- -

THREE COMPREHENSIVE BIENNALE ART MAPS WITH NUMBERED VENUES,
LISTING ALL 90 NATIONAL PAVILIONS AND 21 COLLATERAL EVENTS, PLUS
30 SELECTED GENERAL EXHIBITIONS THAT COINCIDE WITH THE PERIOD

- -

USING THE MAPS

Every exhibition listed in this guide is marked on these maps, making it easy to see at a glance which ones are near to each other, and also the closest waterbus stops. Simply find the show in the alphabetical Exhibition Checklist (pages 22-63) to get the full street address and opening times; or use the Venue Index (pages 118-119) if searching by venue. You can then use an online map to locate the exact position.

VENICE CITY MAP
(PAGES 8-11)

ARSENALE MAP
(PAGE 12)

GIARDINI MAP
(PAGE 13)

The two main Venice Biennale venues are the Giardini with its national pavilions, and the historic Arsenale complex. Top is a Martin Puryear work at the Giardini's USA Pavilion; below is Gaggiandre, the Arsenale's magnificent shipyard.

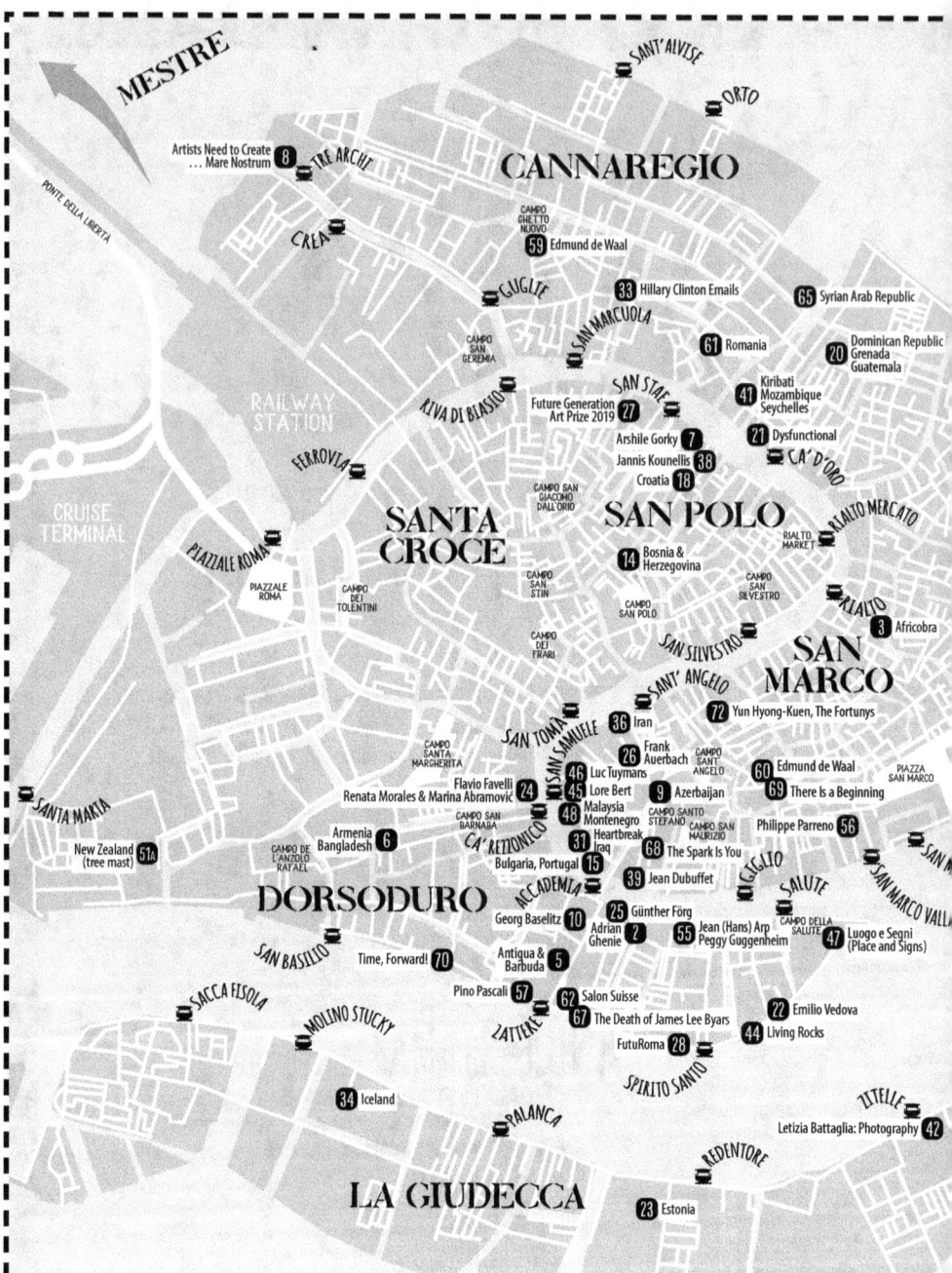

MESTRE

PONTE DELLA LIBERTÀ

Artists Need to Create
... Mare Nostrum **8** TRE ARCHI

CREA

CANNAREGIO

SANT'ALVISE

ORTO

CAMPO GHETTO NUOVO

59 Edmund de Waal

GUGLIE

33 Hillary Clinton Emails

65 Syrian Arab Republic

SAN MARCUOLA

CAMPO SAN GEREMIA

61 Romania

20 Dominican Republic
Grenada
Guatemala

RAILWAY STATION

RIVA DI BIASIO

SAN STAE

Future Generation
Art Prize 2019 **27**

41 Kiribati
Mozambique
Seychelles

21 Dysfunctional

Arshile Gorky **7**

Jannis Kounellis **38**

CA' D'ORO

Croatia **18**

FERROVIA

CRUISE TERMINAL

PIAZZALE ROMA

PIAZZALE ROMA

CAMPO DEI TOLENTINI

CAMPO SAN GIACOMO DALL'ORIO

SANTA
CROCE

SAN POLO

RIALTO MERCATO

RIALTO MARKET

14 Bosnia &
Herzegovina

CAMPO SAN SILVESTRO

RIALTO

3 Africobra

CAMPO SAN STIN

CAMPO SAN POLO

CAMPO DEI FRARI

SAN SILVESTRO

SAN
MARCO

SANT'ANGELO

36 Iran

72 Yun Hyong-Kuen, The Fortunys

SAN TOMA

Frank
Auerbach

26

CAMPO SANT'ANGELO

60 Edmund de Waal

PIAZZA SAN MARCO

SANTA MARTA

CAMPO SANTA MARGHERITA

Flavio Favelli
Renata Morales & Marina Abramović **24**

SAN SAMUELE

46 Luc Tuymans

45 Lore Bert

9 Azerbaijan

69 There Is a Beginning

48 Malaysia
Montenegro

CAMPO SANTO STEFANO

Philippe Parreno **56**

New Zealand
(tree mast) **51A**

Armenia
Bangladesh **6**

CAMPO SAN BARNABA

CA' REZZONICO

31 Heartbreak
Iraq

CAMPO SAN MAURIZIO

68 The Spark Is You

CAMPO DE L'ANZOLO RAFAEL

Bulgaria, Portugal **15**

ACCADEMIA

39 Jean Dubuffet

GIGLIO

SALUTE

DORSODURO

Georg Baselitz **10**

25 Günther Förg

Adrian
Ghenie **2**

55 Jean (Hans) Arp
Peggy Guggenheim

CAMPO DELLA SALUTE

47 Luogo e Segni
(Place and Signs)

SAN MARCO VALLA

SAN BASILIO

Time, Forward! **70**

Antiqua &
Barbuda **5**

SAN M

SACCA FISOLA

MOLINO STUCKY

Pino Pascali **57**

ZATTERE

62 Salon Suisse

67 The Death of James Lee Byars

FutuRoma **28**

22 Emilio Vedova

44 Living Rocks

SPIRITO SANTO

ZITELLE

34 Iceland

PALANCA

REDENTORE

Letizia Battaglia: Photography **42**

LA GIUDECCA

23 Estonia

VENICE CITY MAP

SEE EXHIBITION CHECKLIST
ON PAGES 22-63 FOR FULL
DETAILS OF EACH SHOW

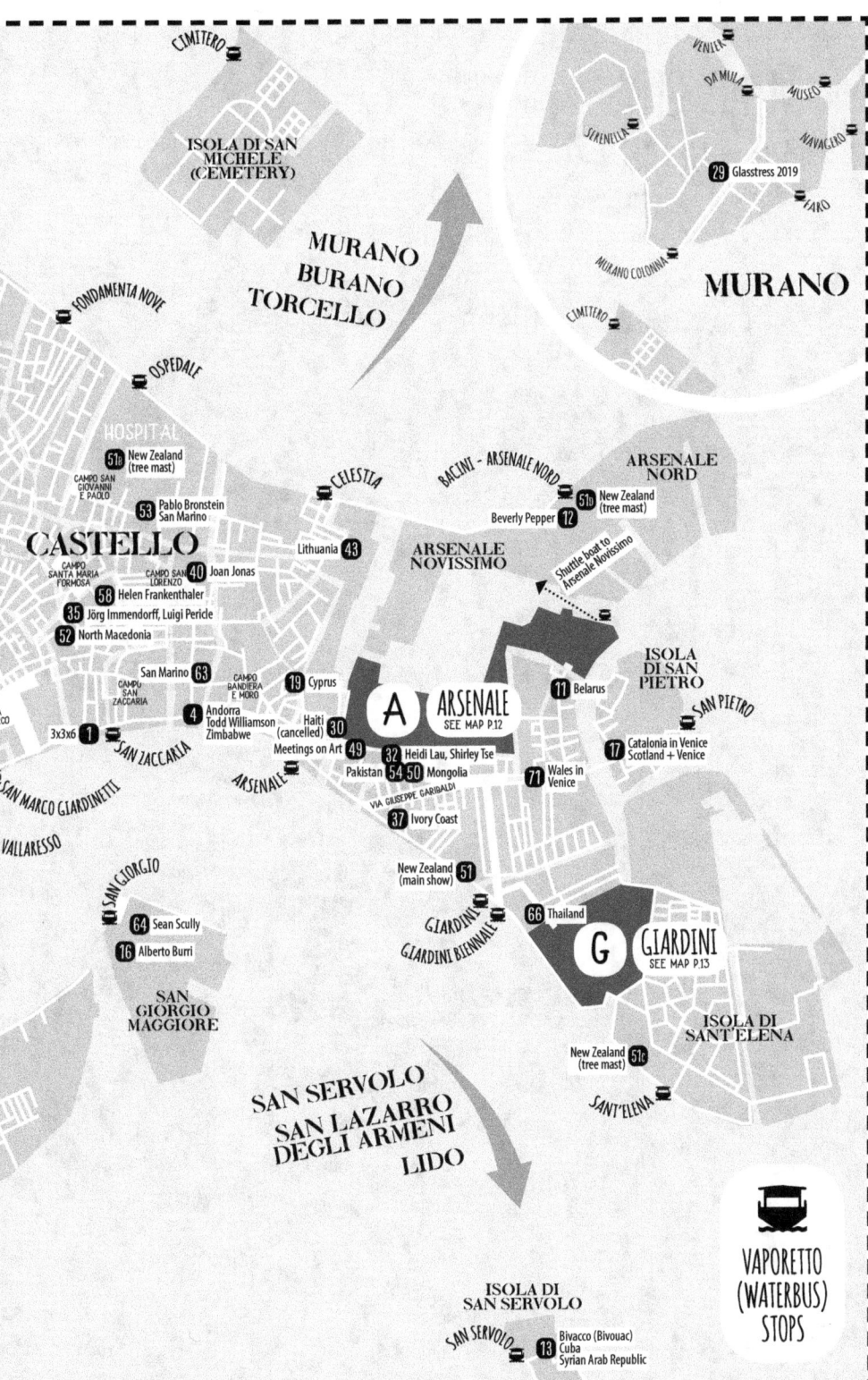

ISOLA DI SAN MICHELE (CEMETERY)

CIMITERO

MURANO BURANO TORCELLO

VENIER

DA MULA

MUSEO

SERENELLA

NAVAGERO

29 Glasstress 2019

FARO

MURANO COLONNA

CIMITERO

MURANO

FONDAMENTA NOVE

OSPEDALE

HOSPITAL

51b New Zealand (tree mast)

CELESTIA

BACINI – ARSENALE NORD

ARSENALE NORD

CAMPO SAN GIOVANNI E PAOLO

53 Pablo Bronstein San Marino

Beverly Pepper 12

51b New Zealand (tree mast)

CASTELLO

CAMPO SANTA MARIA FORMOSA

CAMPO SAN LORENZO 40 Joan Jonas

Lithuania 43

ARSENALE NOVISSIMO

58 Helen Frankenthaler

35 Jörg Immendorff, Luigi Pericle

52 North Macedonia

Shuttle boat to Arsenale Novissimo

ISOLA DI SAN PIETRO

San Marino 63

CAMPU SAN ZACCARIA

CAMPO BANDIERA E MORO

19 Cyprus

11 Belarus

SAN PIETRO

4 Andorra Todd Williamson Zimbabwe

Haiti (cancelled) 30

17 Catalonia in Venice Scotland + Venice

3x3x6 1

SAN ZACCARIA

Meetings on Art 49

32 Heidi Lau, Shirley Tse

71 Wales in Venice

SAN MARCO GIARDINETTI

ARSENALE

Pakistan 54 50 Mongolia

VALLARESSO

VIA GIUSEPPE GARIBALDI

37 Ivory Coast

SAN GIORGIO

New Zealand (main show) 51

64 Sean Scully

GIARDINI

66 Thailand

16 Alberto Burri

GIARDINI BIENNALE

G GIARDINI SEE MAP P.13

SAN GIORGIO MAGGIORE

ISOLA DI SANT'ELENA

New Zealand (tree mast) 51c

SAN SERVOLO SAN LAZZARO DEGLI ARMENI LIDO

SANT'ELENA

VAPORETTO (WATERBUS) STOPS

ISOLA DI SAN SERVOLO

SAN SERVOLO

13 Bivacco (Bivouac) Cuba Syrian Arab Republic

A ARSENALE SEE MAP P.12

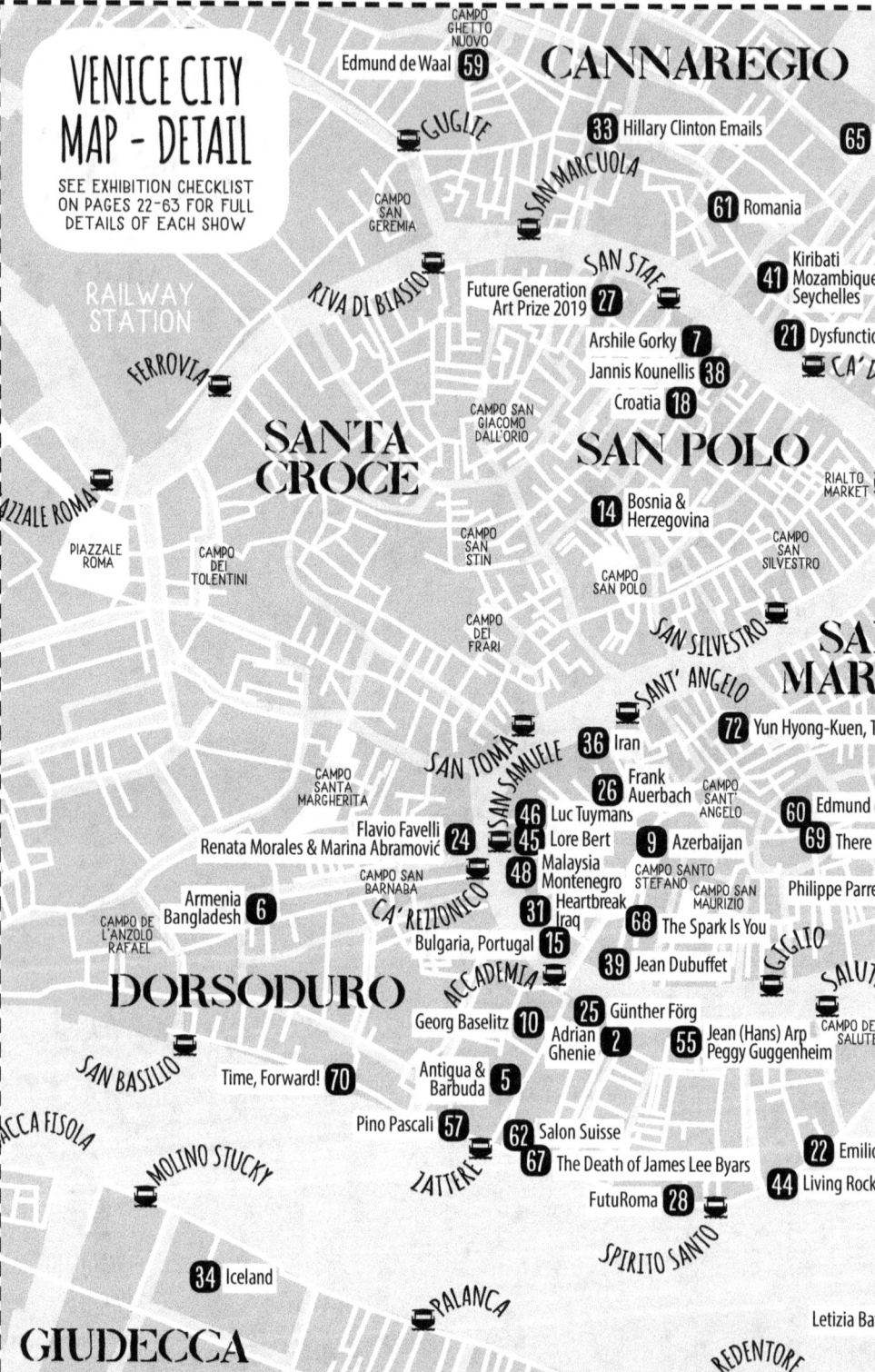

VENICE CITY MAP – DETAIL

SEE EXHIBITION CHECKLIST ON PAGES 22-63 FOR FULL DETAILS OF EACH SHOW

CAMPO GHETTO NUOVO

Edmund de Waal **59**

CANNAREGIO

GUGLIE

33 Hillary Clinton Emails

65 S

SAN MARCUOLA

61 Romania

CAMPO SAN GEREMIA

RIVA DI BIASIO

SAN STAE

41 Kiribati Mozambique Seychelles

Future Generation Art Prize 2019 **27**

21 Dysfunctio

7 Arshile Gorky

CA' D

Jannis Kounellis **38**

Croatia **18**

CAMPO SAN GIACOMO DALL'ORIO

SAN POLO

SANTA CROCE

RAILWAY STATION

FERROVIA

RIALTO MARKET

14 Bosnia & Herzegovina

ZZALE ROMA

CAMPO SAN STIN

CAMPO SAN SILVESTRO

PIAZZALE ROMA

CAMPO DEI TOLENTINI

CAMPO SAN POLO

SAN SILVESTRO

SA

CAMPO DEI FRARI

SANT' ANGELO

MAR

SAN TOMÀ

72 Yun Hyong-Kuen, T

36 Iran

CAMPO SANTA MARGHERITA

SAN SAMUELE

26 Frank Auerbach

CAMPO SANT' ANGELO

60 Edmund d

Flavio Favelli

46 Luc Tuymans

Renata Morales & Marina Abramović **24**

45 Lore Bert

9 Azerbaijan

69 There I

CAMPO SANTO STEFANO

Philippe Parre

CAMPO SAN BARNABA

48 Malaysia Montenegro

CAMPO SAN MAURIZIO

Armenia Bangladesh **6**

CA' REZZONICO

31 Heartbreak Iraq

68 The Spark Is You

CAMPO DE L'ANZOLO RAFAEL

Bulgaria, Portugal **15**

39 Jean Dubuffet

GIGLIO

SALUTE

DORSODURO

ACCADEMIA

25 Günther Förg

Georg Baselitz **10**

2 Adrian Ghenie

55 Jean (Hans) Arp Peggy Guggenheim

CAMPO DEL SALUTE

Time, Forward! **70**

SAN BASILIO

Antiqua & Barbuda **5**

Pino Pascali **57**

62 Salon Suisse

22 Emilio

ACCA FISOLA

MOLINO STUCKY

67 The Death of James Lee Byars

44 Living Rocks

LATTERE

FutuRoma **28**

34 Iceland

SPIRITO SANTO

PALANCA

Letizia Bat

GIUDECCA

REDENTORE

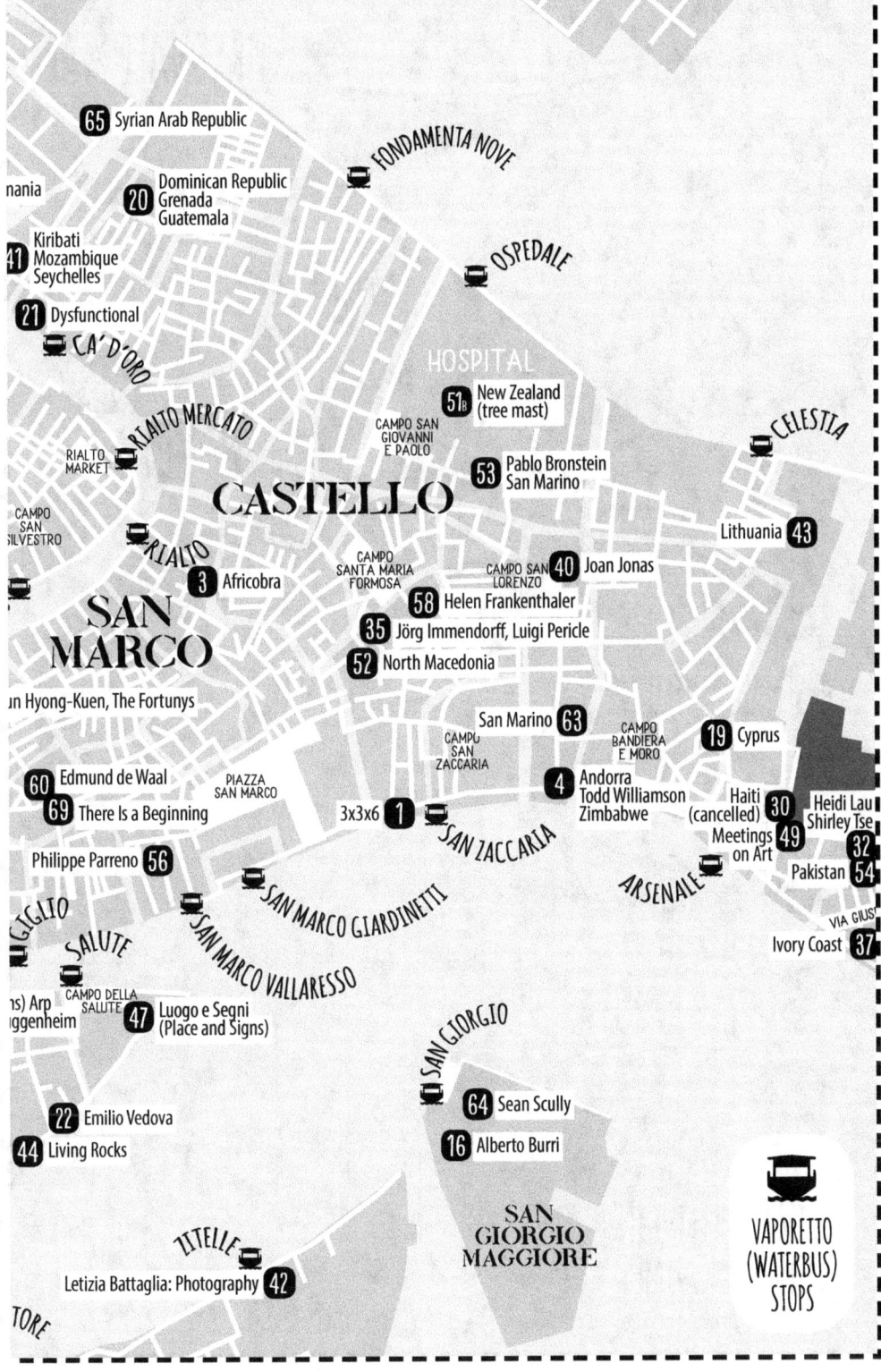

65 Syrian Arab Republic

FONDAMENTA NOVE

20 Dominican Republic
Grenada
Guatemala

nania

OSPEDALE

Kiribati
41 Mozambique
Seychelles

21 Dysfunctional

CA' D'ORO

HOSPITAL

51ᴮ New Zealand
(tree mast)

CAMPO SAN
GIOVANNI
E PAOLO

CELESTIA

RIALTO MERCATO

RIALTO
MARKET

53 Pablo Bronstein
San Marino

CAMPO
SAN
SILVESTRO

CASTELLO

Lithuania 43

RIALTO

CAMPO
SANTA MARIA
FORMOSA

CAMPO SAN
LORENZO

40 Joan Jonas

3 Africobra

58 Helen Frankenthaler

SAN
MARCO

35 Jörg Immendorff, Luigi Pericle

52 North Macedonia

n Hyong-Kuen, The Fortunys

San Marino 63

CAMPO
SAN
ZACCARIA

CAMPO
BANDIERA
E MORO

19 Cyprus

60 Edmund de Waal

PIAZZA
SAN MARCO

69 There Is a Beginning

4 Andorra
Todd Williamson
Zimbabwe

Haiti
30 (cancelled)

Heidi Lau
Shirley Tse

3x3x6 1

SAN ZACCARIA

49 Meetings
on Art

32
54

Philippe Parreno 56

Pakistan

ARSENALE

SAN MARCO GIARDINETTI

GIGIO

VIA GIUS'

SALUTE

SAN MARCO VALLARESSO

Ivory Coast 37

ns) Arp
iggenheim

CAMPO DELLA
SALUTE

47 Luogo e Segni
(Place and Signs)

SAN GIORGIO

22 Emilio Vedova

44 Living Rocks

64 Sean Scully

16 Alberto Burri

ZITELLE

SAN
GIORGIO
MAGGIORE

VAPORETTO
(WATERBUS)
STOPS

Letizia Battaglia: Photography 42

TORE

– 11 –

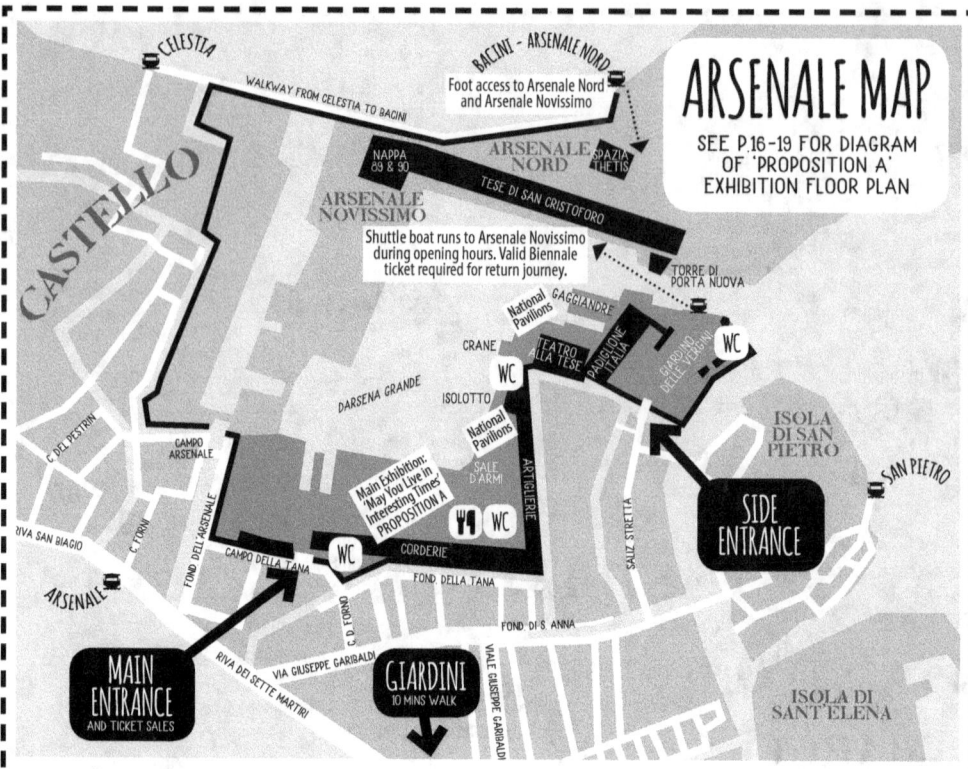

ARSENALE MAP

SEE P.16-19 FOR DIAGRAM OF 'PROPOSITION A' EXHIBITION FLOOR PLAN

CELESTIA

WALKWAY FROM CELESTIA TO BACINI

BACINI - ARSENALE NORD
Foot access to Arsenale Nord and Arsenale Novissimo

CASTELLO

NAPPA 89 & 90

ARSENALE NORD

SPAZIO THETIS

ARSENALE NOVISSIMO

TESE DI SAN CRISTOFORO

Shuttle boat runs to Arsenale Novissimo during opening hours. Valid Biennale ticket required for return journey.

TORRE DI PORTA NUOVA

National Pavilions   GAGGIANDRE

CRANE

TEATRO ALLA TESE   PADIGLIONE ITALIA

WC

GIARDINO DELLE VERGINI

WC

DARSENA GRANDE

ISOLOTTO

National Pavilions

C. DEL PESTRIN

CAMPO ARSENALE

SALE D'ARMI

ARTIGLIERIE

ISOLA DI SAN PIETRO

SAN PIETRO

Main Exhibition: 'May You Live in Interesting Times' PROPOSITION A

C. TORRI

FOND. DELL'ARSENALE

CAMPO DELLA TANA

WC

CORDERIE

WC

SAUZ STRETTA

SIDE ENTRANCE

RIVA SAN BIAGIO

ARSENALE

FOND. DELLA TANA

FOND. DI S. ANNA

RIVA DEI SETTE MARTIRI

VIA GIUSEPPE GARIBALDI

C. D. FORNO

VIALE GIUSEPPE GARIBALDI

MAIN ENTRANCE
AND TICKET SALES

GIARDINI
10 MINS WALK

ISOLA DI SANT'ELENA

ARSENALE PAVILIONS

ALBANIA	MADAGASCAR
ARGENTINA	MALTA
CHILE	MEXICO
CHINA (PEOPLE'S REPUBLIC OF)	PERU
GEORGIA	PHILIPPINES
GHANA	SAUDI ARABIA
INDIA	SINGAPORE
INDONESIA	SLOVENIA (REPUBLIC OF)
IRELAND	
ITALY	SOUTH AFRICA (REPUBLIC OF)
KOSOVO (REPUBLIC OF)	
	TURKEY
LATVIA	UKRAINE
LUXEMBOURG (GRAND DUCHY OF)	UNITED ARAB EMIRATES

+ 'MAY YOU LIVE IN INTERESTING TIMES'
PROPOSITION A

NOTES

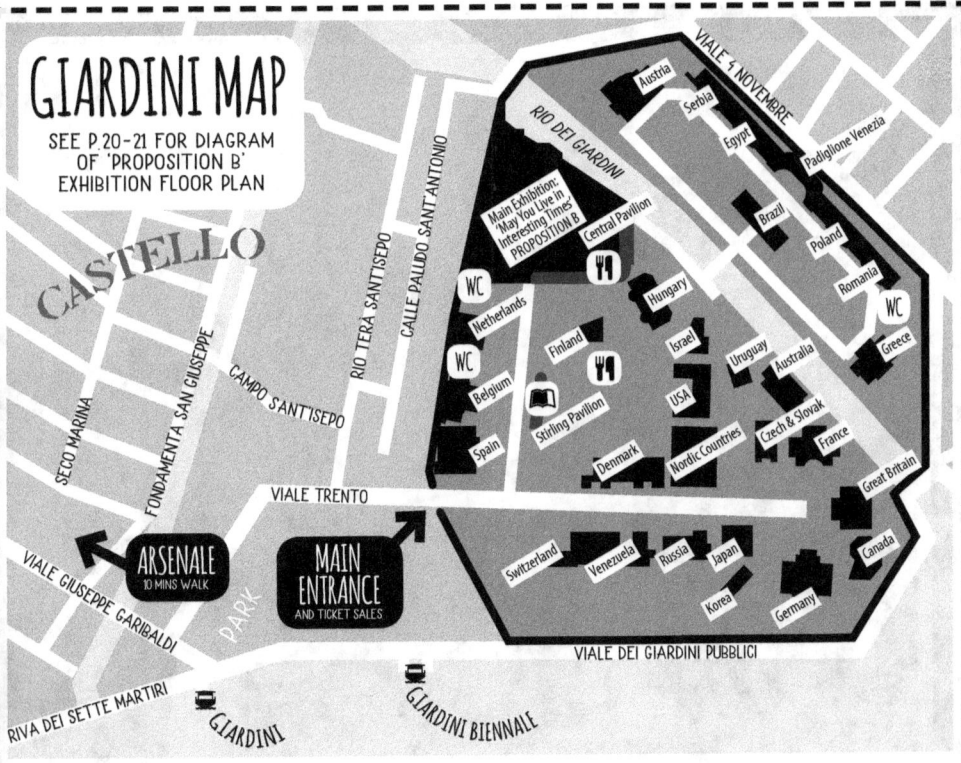

GIARDINI MAP

SEE P.20-21 FOR DIAGRAM
OF 'PROPOSITION B'
EXHIBITION FLOOR PLAN

CASTELLO

RIO DEI GIARDINI

VIALE 4 NOVEMBRE

Austria
Serbia
Egypt
Padiglione Venezia

Main Exhibition:
'May You Live in
Interesting Times'
PROPOSITION B

Central Pavilion

Brazil
Poland
Romania

WC
Netherlands
Hungary
Greece

WC
Finland
Israel
Uruguay
Australia

Belgium
USA
Czech & Slovak
France

Spain
Stirling Pavilion
Denmark
Nordic Countries
Great Britain

RIO TERA SANT'SEPO
CALLE PALUDO SANT'ANTONIO
CAMPO SANT'SEPO
FONDAMENTA SAN GIUSEPPE
SECO MARINA

VIALE TRENTO

Switzerland
Venezuela
Russia
Japan
Canada

Korea
Germany

VIALE GIUSEPPE GARIBALDI

ARSENALE
10 MINS WALK

PARK

MAIN
ENTRANCE
AND TICKET SALES

VIALE DEI GIARDINI PUBBLICI

RIVA DEI SETTE MARTIRI

GIARDINI

GIARDINI BIENNALE

GIARDINI PAVILIONS

AUSTRALIA	JAPAN
AUSTRIA	KOREA (REPUBLIC OF)
BELGIUM	NETHERLANDS (THE)
BRAZIL	NORDIC COUNTRIES
CANADA	(FINLAND, NORWAY, SWEDEN)
CZECH (REPUBLIC) & SLOVAK (REPUBLIC)	POLAND
DENMARK	ROMANIA
EGYPT	RUSSIA
FINLAND (ALVAR AALTO PAVILION)	SERBIA
FRANCE	SPAIN
GERMANY	SWITZERLAND
GREAT BRITAIN	UNITED STATES OF AMERICA
GREECE	URUGUAY
HUNGARY	VENEZUELA (BOLIVARIAN REPUBLIC OF)
ISRAEL	

+ 'MAY YOU LIVE IN INTERESTING TIMES'
PROPOSITION B

NOTES

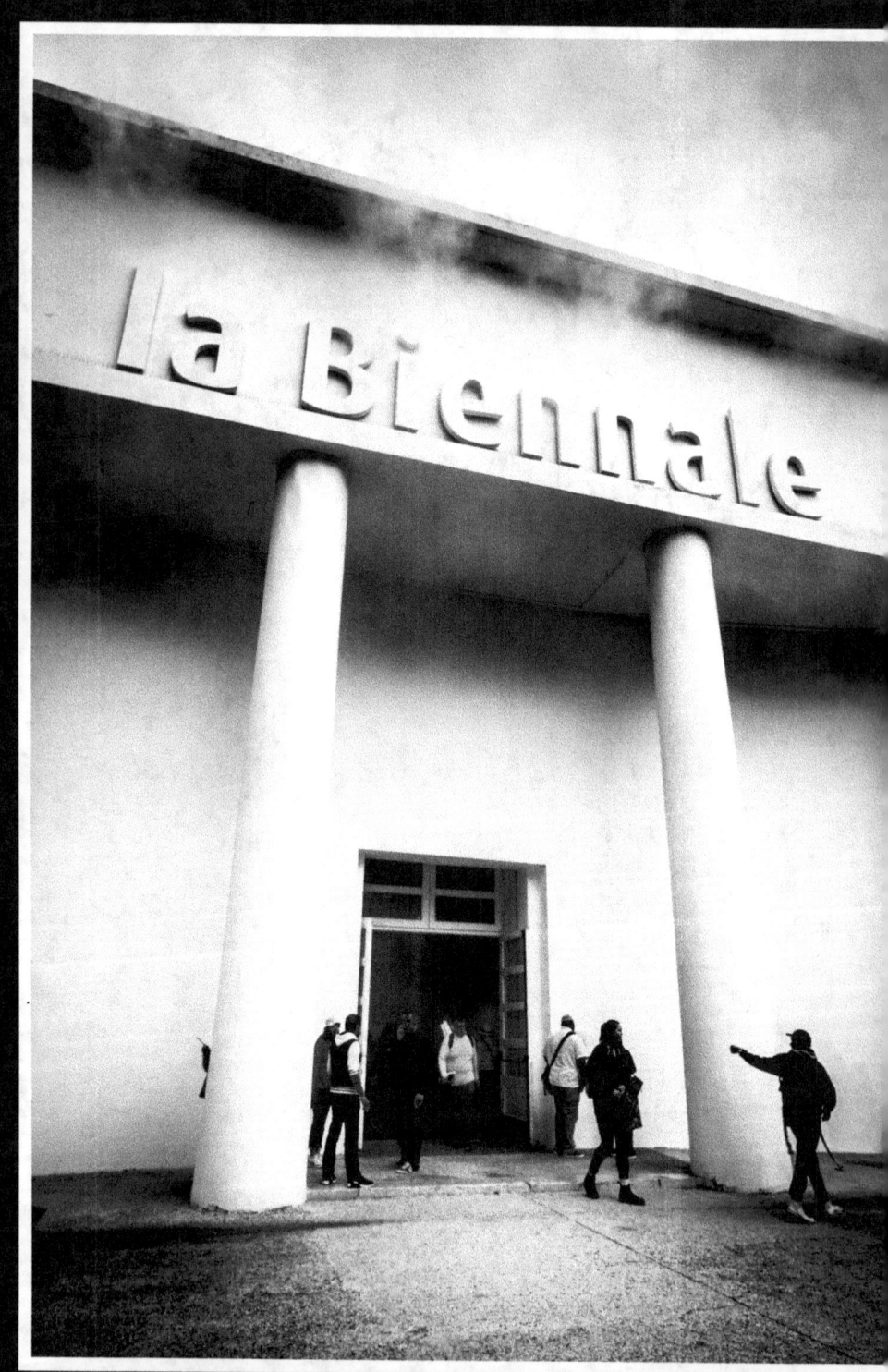

Main Show
FLOOR PLANS

'MAY YOU LIVE IN INTERESTING TIMES'
PROPOSITION A (ARSENALE) + PROPOSITION B (GIARDINI)
PLUS ARSENALE NATIONAL PAVILIONS

USING THE FLOOR PLANS

These diagrams show the layout of the Ralph Rugoff-curated central exhibition, 'May You Live in Interesting Times', at each of its two sites. Also included are the Arsenale's 2019 national pavilions, some of which vary with each Biennale. Numbered keys give the location of each participant.

ARSENALE: PROPOSITION A + PAVILIONS
(PAGES 16–19)

GIARDINI: PROPOSITION B
(PAGES 20–21)

The Giardini's central pavilion — home to Proposition B — wreathed in a misty work by Lara Favaretto, 'Thinking Head, 2017-2019' (2019)

ARSENALE
CORDERIE, ARTIGLIERIE

ARTISTS

01	George Condo	19	Darren Bader	36	Rula Halawani
02	Anthony Hernandez	20	Nabuqi	37	Julie Mehretu
03	Soham Gupta	21	Martine Gutierrez	38	Otobong Nkanga
04	Christian Marclay	22	Jill Mulleady	39	Lawrence Abu Hamdan
05	Zanele Muholi	23	Carol Bove	40	Gauri Gill
06	Ed Atkins	24	Suki Seokyeong Kang	41	Michael Armitage
07	Tavares Strachan	25	Korakrit Arunanondchai and Alex Gvojic	42	Ulrike Müller
08	Gabriel Rico			43	Haris Epaminonda
09	Kahlil Joseph	26	Jean-Luc Moulène	44	Dominique Gonzalez-Foerster
10	Shilpa Gupta	27	Handiwirman Saputra	45	Yu Ji
11	Henry Taylor	28	Mari Katayama	46	Jesse Darling
12	Augustas Serapinas	29	Nicole Eisenman	47	Rosemarie Trockel
13	Teresa Margolles	30	Lee Bul	48	Michael E. Smith
14	Apichatpong Weerasethakuland and Tsuyoshi Hisakado	31	Kaari Upson	49	Liu Wei
		32	Sun Yuan & Peng Yu	50	Alexandra Bircken
15	Njideka Akunyili Crosby	33	Cameron Jamie	51	Alex Da Corte
16	Kemang Wa Lehulere	34	Hito Steyerl	52	Frida Orupabo
17	Stan Douglas	35	Christine and Margaret Wertheim	53	Ad Minoliti
18	Yin Xiuzhen			54	Antoine Catala

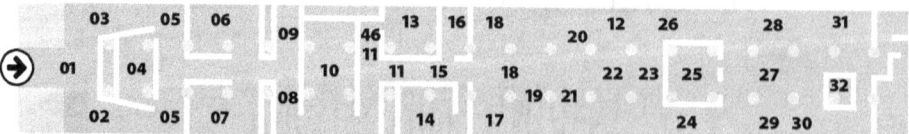

CORDERIE

PROPOSITION A

'MAY YOU LIVE IN INTERESTING TIMES'

KEY

55 Khyentse Norbu	AED Defibrillator
56 Jon Rafman	Biennale Educational
57 Ian Cheng	Bookshop
58 Anthea Hamilton	Cloakroom
59 Avery Singer	Courtesy Stroller
60 Arthur Jafa	Entrance / Exit
61 Lara Favaretto	Family Area
62 Andra Ursuţa	First Aid
63 Neïl Beloufa	Information Point
64 Ryoji Ikeda	Press Office
65 Danh Vo	Restaurant
66 Tarek Atoui	Snacks
67 Jimmie Durham	Ticket Office
68 Anicka Yi	Toilets
69 Zhanna Kadyrova	Wifi Point
70 Maria Loboda	
71 Slavs and Tatars	

MULTIPLE LOCATIONS

Zanele Muholi

**EXHIBITION
CONTINUES**
(SEE NEXT PAGE)

ARTIGLIERIE

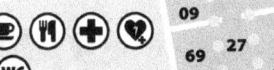

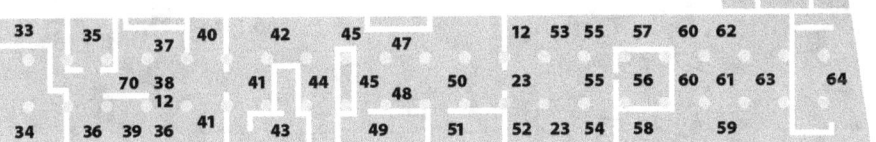

CORDERIE

ARSENALE

GAGGIANDRE, GIARDRINO DELLE VERGINI

ARTISTS

72 Nairy Baghramian

73 Christoph Büchel

74 Ludovica Carbotta

75 Tomás Saraceno

76 Halil Altındere

77 Andreas Lolis

78 Cyprien Gaillard

79 Michael E. Smith

80 Posters for Alternative Biennales

SPECIAL PROJECTS

ARSENALE (PAA)

Marysia Lewandowska
'It's About Time' (2019)

Pavilion of Applied Arts – La Biennale di Venezia with Victoria and Albert Museum

MESTRE (OFF MAP)

Ludovica Carbotta
'Monowe (The Powder Room)' (2019)

Forte Marghera, Polveriera Austriaca (Austrian Gunpowder Store),
Via Forte Marghera 30, Mestre

7 May-6 Oct 2019, 13:00-21:00, closed Mon

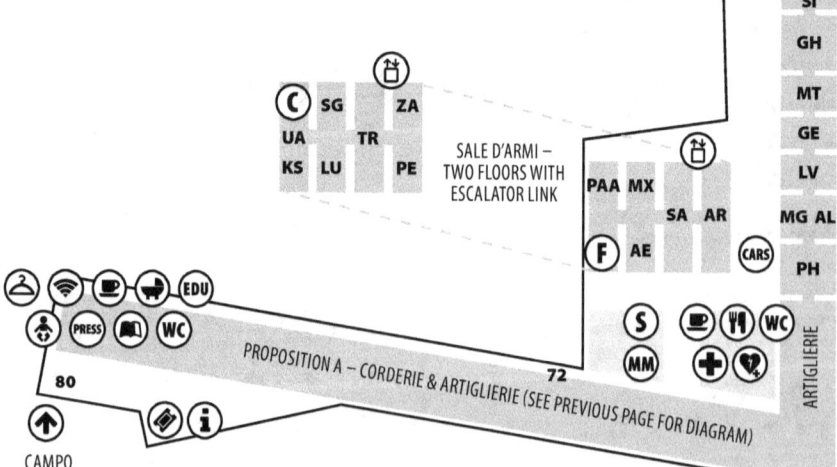

MAIN SHOW FLOOR PLANS

PROPOSITION A

(CONTINUED) PLUS NATIONAL PAVILIONS

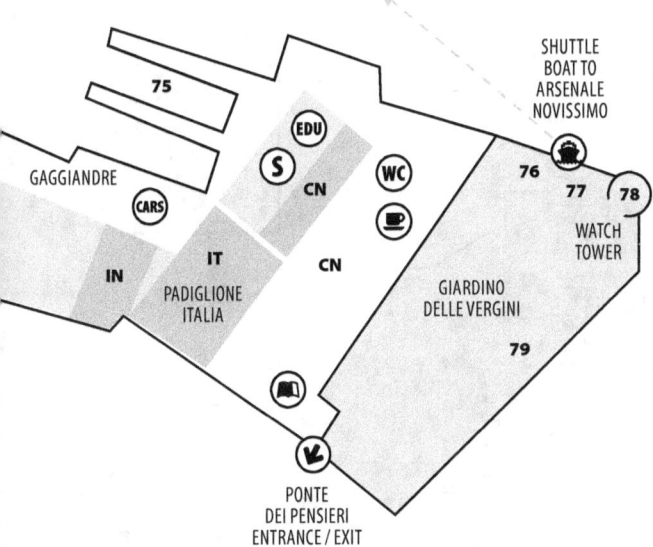

SHUTTLE BOAT TO ARSENALE NOVISSIMO

GAGGIANDRE

EDU

S

CN

WC

CARS

IT

PADIGLIONE ITALIA

IN

CN

76

77 78

WATCH TOWER

GIARDINO DELLE VERGINI

79

PONTE DEI PENSIERI ENTRANCE / EXIT

75

KEY

- 🫀 AED Defibrillator
- Ⓒ Biennale College
- (EDU) Biennale Educational
- Ⓢ Biennale Sessions
- 📖 Bookshop
- 👔 Cloakroom
- 🛒 Courtesy Stroller
- ➔ Entrance / Exit
- 👨‍👦 Family Area
- ➕ First Aid
- ⓘ Information Point
- 🛗 Lift / Escalator
- (MM) Multimedia Music Information Centre
- (PRESS) Press Office
- 🍴 Restaurant
- ⛴ Shuttle Boat
- (CARS) Shuttle Cars
- ☕ Snacks
- Ⓕ Swatch Faces 2019: The Swatch Art Peace Hotel
- 🎫 Ticket Office
- (WC) Toilets
- 📶 Wifi Point

PAVILIONS

AL Albania	**GH** Ghana	**MT** Malta
SA Saudi Arabia	**LU** Grand Duchy of Luxembourg	**MX** Mexico
AR Argentina		**PE** Peru
CL Chile	**IN** India	**SG** Singapore
CN People's Republic of China	**ID** Indonesia	**SI** Republic of Slovenia
	IE Ireland	**ZA** Republic of South Africa
AE United Arab Emirates	**IT** Italy	**TR** Turkey
PH Philippines	**KS** Republic of Kosovo	**UA** Ukraine
GE Georgia	**LV** Latvia	
	MG Madagascar	

GIARDINI
CENTRAL PAVILION

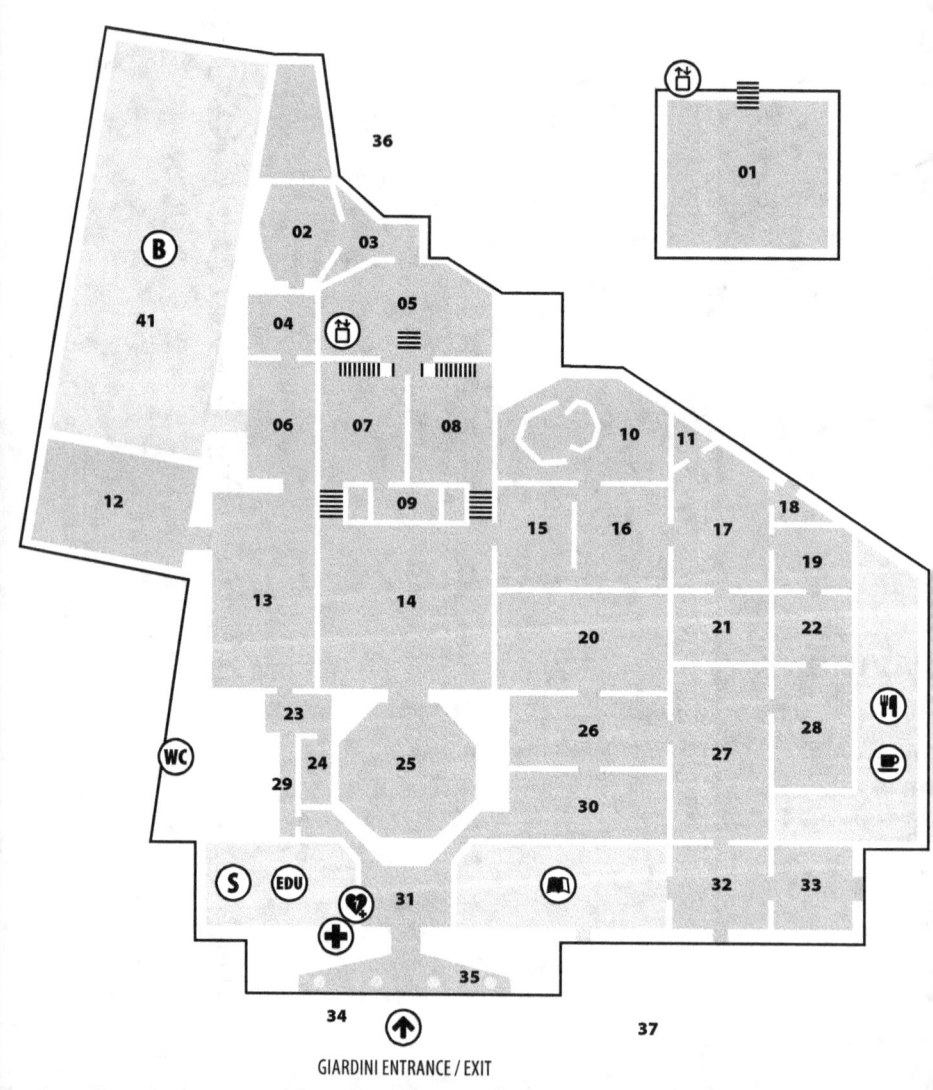

GIARDINI ENTRANCE / EXIT

PROPOSITION B
'MAY YOU LIVE IN INTERESTING TIMES'

ARTISTS

01 Nairy Baghramian
George Condo
Jimmie Durham
Julie Mehretu
Henry Taylor
02 Arthur Jafa
03 Neïl Beloufa
04 Jon Rafman
05 Ian Cheng
Zhanna Kadyrova
Jill Mulleady
06 Martine Gutierrez
Ad Minoliti
Ulrike Müller
Kaari Upson
07 Lee Bul
Soham Gupta
Rula Halawani
08 Lawrence Abu Hamdan
09 Lara Favaretto
10 Michael Armitage
Jesse Darling
Gauri Gill
Khyentse Norbu
Kemang Wa Lehulere
11 Christine and Margaret Wertheim
12 Michael E. Smith

13 Nicole Eisenman
Cameron Jamie
Jean-Luc Moulène
Augustas Serapinas
Rosemarie Trockel
14 Christian Marclay
Teresa Margolles
Frida Orupabo
Sun Yuan and Peng Yu
15 Liu Wei
Handiwirman Saputra
Slavs and Tatars
16 Alexandra Bircken
17 Shilpa Gupta
Nabuqi
18 Apichatpong Weerasethakul
19 Hito Steyerl
20 Stan Douglas
21 Suki Seokyeong Kang
Otobong Nkanga
22 Alex Da Corte
23 Darren Bader
24 Haris Epaminonda
25 Cyprien Gaillard
Danh Vo
Yu Ji
26 Mari Katayama
Zanele Muholi

27 Njideka Akunyili Crosby
Carol Bove
Anthony Hernandez
Avery Singer
28 Halil Altındere
Dominique Gonzalez-Foerster and Joi Bittle
Yin Xiuzhen
29 Ryoji Ikeda
30 Korakrit Arunanondchai
Gabriel Rico
Tavares Strachan
31 Antoine Catala
32 Anicka Yi
33 Kahlil Joseph
Anthea Hamilton
34 Lara Favaretto
35 Andreas Lolis
36 Zhanna Kadyrova
37 Tomás Saraceno

MULTIPLE LOCATIONS
Andra Ursuţa
Apichatpong Weerasethakul
Ed Atkins
Maria Loboda

KEY

🏥 AED Defibrillator
EDU Biennale Educational
B Biennale Library
S Biennale Sessions
📖 Bookshop
→ Entrance / Exit
✚ First Aid
Lift / Escalator
🍴 Restaurant
☕ Snacks
≡ Stairs
WC Toilets

GIARDINI GROUNDS (SEE ALSO MAP P.13)

38 Jeppe Hein *(between Brazil and Greece)*
39 Maria Loboda *(Stirling Pavilion)*
40 Tarek Atoui *(Stirling Pavilion)*
41 Posters for Alternative Biennales *(Stirling Pavilion / Biennale Library)*
42 Anthea Hamilton *(Stirling Pavilion)*

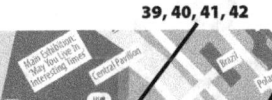

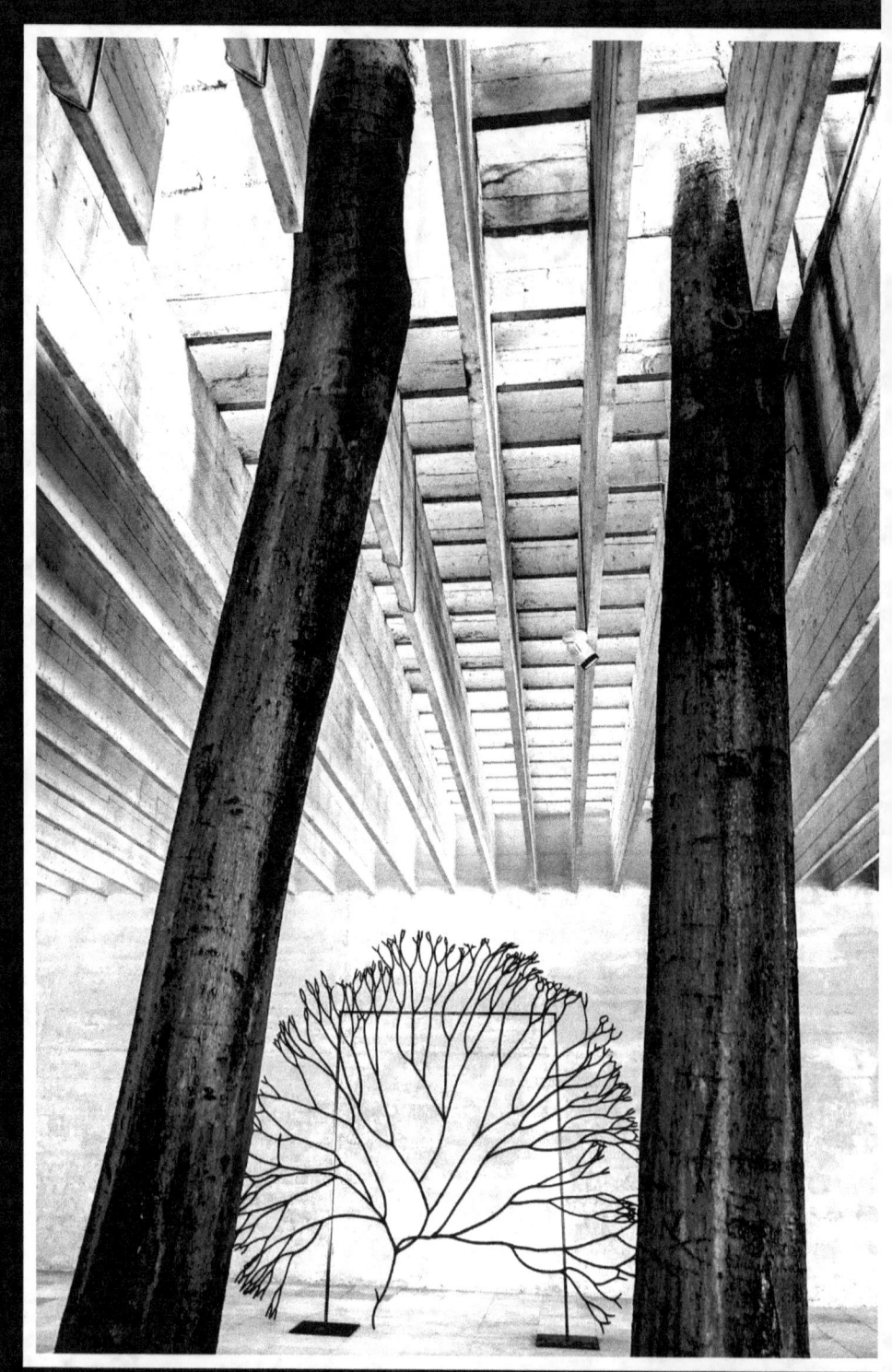

EXHIBITION CHECKLIST

FOR THE 2019 / 58TH VENICE ART BIENNALE

- -

LISTED IN ALPHABETIAL ORDER, WITH SPACE FOR NOTES: ALL 90 OFFICIAL
NATIONAL PAVILIONS AND 21 COLLATERAL EVENTS, PLUS 30 SELECTED
GENERAL EXHIBITIONS THAT COINCIDED WITH THE BIENNALE

- -

USING THE CHECKLIST

All the useful details are in one spot: the pavilion and exhibition title, opening details, artists, show description, map key number and address. NATIONAL PAVILIONS and COLLATERAL EVENTS are official Biennale shows, while GENERAL EXHIBITIONS are independent shows that ran alongside the Biennale.

Every exhibition is listed in alphabetical order of title. The next columns give a list of artists in each show, plus concise descriptions of what it comprised – a helpful reminder, when there was so much to see.

On the right is the street address, and a key number. This refers to the maps, whose page numbers are given above the listings. You can then see at a glance where the exhibition was, and others nearby.

This is followed by a column for personal notes, plus check-boxes to tick off what you've seen.

- - - MAPS - - -
VENICE CITY MAP (P.8-11) ARSENALE MAP (P.12) GIARDINI MAP (P.13)

Trees growing inside the Nordic Pavilion frame part of Ingela Ihrman's algae installation 'A Great Seaweed Day' (2018-2019)

Exhibition Checklist

ALL 90 NATIONAL PAVILIONS & 21 COLLATERAL EVENTS + 30 SELECTED EXHIBITIONS

PAVILION / EXHIBITION	DETAILS	ARTISTS	DESCRIPTION
3X3X6	Collateral Event **11 MAY-24 NOV 2019** 10:00-18:00, closed Mon **FREE ENTRY**	CHEANG SHU-LEA	The first female artist selected to represent Taiwan, Cheang Shu-Lea is a pioneer of 'net art', which involves the viewer in digital spaces and online activities. Held in a former jail, this show explored themes of imprisonment and surveillance. The title refers to a nine-metre-square prison cell monitored by six cameras.
ADRIAN GHENIE: THE BATTLE BETWEEN CARNIVAL AND FEAST	General Exhibition **19 APR-18 NOV 2019** 11:00-19:00 (ticket office closes 18:15), closed Tue **PAID ENTRY**	ADRIAN GHENIE	A suite of specially created paintings inspired by Dutch painter Pieter Bruegel the Elder's 'Battle between Carnival and Lent', which referenced the Venice carnival, plus significant historical figures. The beautiful venue was once the home of a major industrialist and art collector.
AFRICOBRA: NATION TIME	Collateral Event **11 MAY-24 NOV 2019** 10:00-18:00, closed Mon **FREE ENTRY**	JEFF DONALDSON, GERALD WILLIAMS, JAE JARRELL, WADSWORTH JARRELL, BARBARA JONES-HOGU, NAPOLEON JONES-HENDERSON, NELSON STEVENS	Focusing on the history of Africobra, a collective of young black artists founded in Chicago in 1968, this impressive and wide-ranging survey majored on paintings and sculpture, including over 40 works plus archive material.
ALBANIA MAYBE THE COSMOS IS NOT SO EXTRAORDINARY	National Pavilion **11 MAY-24 NOV 2019** 10:00-18:00 (10:00-20:00 Fri & Sat until 5 Oct), closed Mon (except 13 May, 2 Sep, 18 Nov) **PAID ENTRY (BIENNALE TICKET)**	DRIANT ZENELI	A film installation set in the chrome mines of Bulqize, north-east Albania, in which a group of teenagers discover a cosmic capsule and follow its journey to worldwide exploitation. Inspired by 'On the Way to Epsilon Eridani', a 1983 sci-fi novel by Albanian physicist Arion Hysenbegas, it is part of a larger multi-disciplinary project, 'Beneath a surface there is just another surface'.
ANDORRA THE FUTURE IS NOW / EL FUTUR ÉS ARA	National Pavilion **11 MAY-24 NOV 2019** 10:00-18:00, closed Mon **FREE ENTRY**	PHILIPPE SHANGTI	Fragmentary, neon-hued multimedia installation by a French-born photographer and artist. The disparate array of large, meticulously crafted elements riffed on consumerism past, present, and future, all presented with a kitsch, camp playfulness that harked back to pop and graffiti art.
ANTIGUA & BARBUDA FIND YOURSELF: CARNIVAL AND RESISTANCE	National Pavilion **11 MAY-24 NOV 2019** 10:00-18:00, closed Mon **FREE ENTRY**	TIMOTHY PAYNE, SIR GERALD PRICE, JOSEPH SETON, AND FRANK WALTER: INTANGIBLE CULTURAL, HERITAGE ARTISANS & MAS TROUP	A multimedia exploration of Carnival around the world, from its roots in slavery to its current-day glamour and popularity. The form's African heritage, and the army of craftspeople who maintain it, was powerfully evidenced in stunning photos, art, masks and costumes.
ARGENTINA EL NOMBRE DE UN PAÍS / THE NAME OF A COUNTRY	National Pavilion **11 MAY-24 NOV 2019** 10:00-18:00 (10:00-20:00 Fri & Sat until 5 Oct), closed Mon (except 13 May, 2 Sep, 18 Nov) **PAID ENTRY (BIENNALE TICKET)**	MARIANA TELLERIA	Seven monumental sculptures with a gothic, post-apocalyptic feel inhabited this cavernous Arsenale space. Dark, menacing shapes loomed spotlit in the gloom, suggesting heavy metal Frankenstein's monsters. References to religion, trash, fashion, and nature were included in the mix.

- - - - - KEY - - - - -

123 VENICE CITY MAP (P.8-11) **A** ARSENALE MAP (P.12) **G** GIARDINI MAP (P.13)

MAP KEY	ADDRESS	NOTES	TICK IF SEEN
1	Palazzo delle Prigioni, Riva degli Schiavoni, Castello 4209		◯
2	Palazzo Cini Gallery, Campo San Vio, Dorsoduro 864		◯
3	Ca'Faccanon (Central Post Office), San Marco 5016		◯
A	Arsenale		◯
4	Istituto Santa Maria della Pietà, Calle de la Pietà, Castello 3701		◯
5	Centro Culturale Don Orione Artigianelli, Dorsoduro 919		◯
A	Arsenale		◯

CONTINUES OVER »

EXHIBITION CHECKLIST

ALL 90 NATIONAL PAVILIONS & 21 COLLATERAL EVENTS + 30 SELECTED EXHIBITIONS

>> ARMENIA TO BANGLADESH

PAVILION / EXHIBITION	DETAILS	ARTISTS	DESCRIPTION
ARMENIA (REPUBLIC OF) REVOLUTIONARY SENSORIUM	National Pavilion 11 MAY-24 NOV 2019 10:00-18:00, closed Mon **FREE ENTRY**	'ARTLABYEREVAN' ARTISTIC GROUP (GAGIK CHARCHYAN, HOVHANNES MARGARYAN, ARTHUR PETROSYAN, VARDAN JALOYAN) & NARINE ARAKELIAN	A data-oriented research project by ArtLab Yerevan, examining Armenia's 'velvet revolution' of spring 2018, and relating it to Armenia's needs today. The three-part show included large-scale video, discussions, and a 50-woman volunteer team recreating female civil disobedience acts of the era around Venice.
ARSHILE GORKY: 1904 – 1948	General Exhibition 8 MAY-22 SEP 2019 10:00-18:00, closed Mon **PAID ENTRY**	ARSHILE GORKY	A selection of Gorky's paintings and works on paper, on loan from major international donors. The venue's permanent collection includes modern Italian and international art, plus the atmospheric Museum of Oriental Art, home to many important Japanese artefacts.
ARTISTS NEED TO CREATE ON THE SAME SCALE THAT SOCIETY HAS THE CAPACITY TO DESTROY: MARE NOSTRUM	Collateral Event 8 MAY-24 NOV 2019 10:00-18:00, closed Mon **FREE ENTRY**	GROUP SHOW OF 73 INTERNATIONAL ARTISTS	An exhibition of works responding to climate change, with 73 major artists ranging from Peter Acheson to Lisa Yuskavage. It was organised by arts publication 'The Brooklyn Rail', and named after a neon piece by Lauren Bon. Also featured a multi-disciplinary programme called '1001 Stories for Survival', which included music, poetry, and free public discussions with scientists, writers, and artists.
AUSTRALIA ASSEMBLY	National Pavilion 11 MAY-24 NOV 2019 10:00-18:00, closed Mon (except 13 May, 2 Sep, 18 Nov) **PAID ENTRY (BIENNALE TICKET)**	ANGELICA MESITI	Visitors sat in a democratic circle to watch this beautifully shot and multi-layered video installation. The film includes a poem coded from a vintage stenographic device used in Italy's parliament, and a soundtrack based on it that moves from cacophony to harmony. As a camera travels through 'the architecture of power', namely Italy and Australia's senate chambers, groups of multi-ethnic people gather, disassemble and re-unite.
AUSTRIA DISCORDO ERGO SUM	National Pavilion 11 MAY-24 NOV 2019 10:00-18:00, closed Mon (except 13 May, 2 Sep, 18 Nov) **PAID ENTRY (BIENNALE TICKET)**	RENATE BERTLMANN	In the pavilion's courtyard, 312 blood-red glass objects were speared upon slim metallic stalks, arrayed with military precision. At first glance, these 'knife roses' appeared to be hearts, but upon closer inspection resembled uteruses. Inside the pavilion was a minimalist back-and-white display, surveying the artist's radical feminist practice of the 1970s and 80s.
AZERBAIJAN (REPUBLIC OF) VIRTUAL REALITY	National Pavilion 11 MAY-24 NOV 2019 10:00-18:00, closed Mon **FREE ENTRY**	ZEIGAM AZIZOV, ORKHAN MAMMADOV, ZARNISHAN YUSIFOVA, KANAN ALIYEV, ULVIYYA ALIYEVA	A group show of interactive multimedia works exploring the 'fake news bubble'. Included a globe of hands that changed direction at the slightest interference, and a crowd of worried-looking mannequins joined at the head by giant Slinky-style springs, representing the news flow from social networks (both by Aliyev and Aliyeva).
BANGLADESH (PEOPLE'S REPUBLIC OF) THIRST	National Pavilion 11 MAY-24 NOV 2019 10:00-18:00, closed Mon **FREE ENTRY**	BISHWAJIT GOSWAMI, DILARA BEGUM JOLLY, HEIDI FOSLI, NAFIS AHMED GAZI, FRANCO MARROCCO, DOMENICO PELLEGRINO, PREEMA NAZIA ANDALEEB, RA KAJOL, UTTAM KUMAR KARMAKER	Artists whose nation suffers both flooding and drought presented five stages of water: crisis, intuition, hope, knowledge, and purification.

- - - - - KEY - - - - -

123 VENICE CITY MAP (P.8-11) **A** ARSENALE MAP (P.12) **G** GIARDINI MAP (P.13)

MAP KEY	ADDRESS	NOTES	TICK IF SEEN
6	Palazzo Zenobio – Collegio Armeno Moorat-Raphael, Fondamenta Soccorso, Dorsoduro 2596		◯
7	Ca' Pesaro, International Gallery of Modern Art, Santa Croce 2076		◯
8	Chiesa di Santa Maria delle Penitenti, Fondamenta Cannaregio, Cannaregio 910		◯
G	Giardini		◯
G	Giardini		◯
9	Palazzo Lezze, Campo Santo Stefano, San Marco 2949		◯
6	Palazzo Zenobio – Collegio Armeno Moorat-Raphael, Fondamenta Soccorso, Dorsoduro 2596		◯

CONTINUES OVER »

Exhibition Checklist

ALL 90 NATIONAL PAVILIONS & 21 COLLATERAL EVENTS + 30 SELECTED EXHIBITIONS

PAVILION / EXHIBITION	DETAILS	ARTISTS	DESCRIPTION
BASELITZ – ACADEMY	COLLATERAL EVENT **8 MAY-6 OCT 2019** 08:15-14:00 Mon, 08:15-19:15 Tue-Sun **PAID ENTRY**	GEORG BASELITZ	Major retrospective of this leading figurative painter and sculptor's 60-year career. It was the first such contemporary survey in the Accademia, which is usually celebrated for its Venetian and historic masterpieces.
BELARUS (REPUBLIC OF) EXIT / USCITA	NATIONAL PAVILION **11 MAY-24 NOV 2019** 11:00-13:00, 14:00-18:00, closed Mon **FREE ENTRY**	KONSTANTIN SELIKHANOV	Five life-sized, faceless human figures, representing different depersonalised states, adopted different stances such as crouching and floating. Each was incorporated with another object, including a screen of static, a neon 'Open' sign, packing crates, and a tray of milk glasses.
BELGIUM MONDO CANE	NATIONAL PAVILION **11 MAY-24 NOV 2019** 10:00-18:00, closed Mon (except 13 May, 2 Sep, 18 Nov) **PAID ENTRY (BIENNALE TICKET)**	JOS DE GRUYTER & HARALD THYS	The pavilion was filled with a quirky crowd of automated, life-sized puppets, all painstakingly styled and dressed. Central was a utopian scene, with artists and craftspeople demonstrating their skills. Round the edge lurked a parallel world of misfits and drop-outs; the groups were clearly segregated, and seemingly unaware of each other.
BEVERLY PEPPER: ART IN THE OPEN	COLLATERAL EVENT **11 MAY-24 NOV 2019** 10:00-18:00, closed Mon **FREE ENTRY**	BEVERLY PEPPER	This American artist, born in 1922, first made massive Cor-ten steel objects in 1964, before Richard Serra. (She also happens to be the mother of Pulitzer Prize-winning poet Jorie Graham.) The show was part of Pepper's ongoing project working towards a sculpture park, and included her monumental steel 'Todi Columns' from 1979, plus two recent sculptures, photos, and preparatory works.
BIVACCO (BIVOUAC)	GENERAL EXHIBITION **11 MAY-30 SEP 2019** 12:00-23:00 daily **FREE ENTRY**	JACOPO CANDOTTI, NICOLÒ DEGIORGIS, HANNES EGGER, JULIA FRANK, SIMON PERATHONER, LEANDER SCHÖNWEGER AND MARIA WALCHER	An emergency high mountain shelter, or bivouac, housed the unofficial 'Pavilion of South Tyrol'. Inside was a group show, positing the area as a land of transit, borders, exchange, and welcome.
BOSNIA & HERZEGOVINA ZENICA TRILOGY	NATIONAL PAVILION **11 MAY-24 NOV 2019** 10:00-18:00, closed Mon **FREE ENTRY**	DANICA DAKIĆ	The Bosnian-Herzegovinian city of Zenica once had one of Europe's largest steel works, and was seen in the former Yugoslavia as a symbol of progress. Involving residents of both Zenica and Sarajevo, this film trilogy explored its reality since the Bosian war, including unemployment, air pollution, and a sense of hopelessness.
BRAZIL SWINGUERRA	NATIONAL PAVILION **11 MAY-24 NOV 2019** 10:00-18:00, closed Mon (except 13 May, 2 Sep, 18 Nov) **PAID ENTRY (BIENNALE TICKET)**	BÁRBARA WAGNER & BENJAMIN DE BURCA	A pun on the popular dance movement swingueira, and the word guerra, meaning war, this video posited dance styles popular with Brazil's queer and trans subcultures — swingueira, brega funk, passinhos de maloca — as a kind of cultural battle. Presented in the energetic style of a music documentary, it also included portraits of the participants.

- - - - - KEY - - - - -

123 VENICE CITY MAP (P.8-11)   A ARSENALE MAP (P.12)   G GIARDINI MAP (P.13)

MAP KEY	ADDRESS	NOTES	TICK IF SEEN
10	Gallerie dell' Accademia, Campo della Carità, Dorsoduro 1050		◯
11	Spazio Liquido, Salizada Streta, Castello 103		◯
G	Giardini		◯
12	Spazia Thetis, Arsenale Novissimo, Castello 2737/F		◯
13	Isola di San Servolo		◯
14	Palazzo Francesco Molon Ca' Bernardo, San Polo 2184/A		◯
G	Giardini		◯

CONTINUES OVER »

Exhibition Checklist

ALL 90 NATIONAL PAVILIONS & 21 COLLATERAL EVENTS + 30 SELECTED EXHIBITIONS

PAVILION / EXHIBITION	DETAILS	ARTISTS	DESCRIPTION
BULGARIA HOW WE LIVE	National Pavilion **11 MAY–24 NOV 2019** 10:00–18:00, closed Mon **FREE ENTRY**	RADA BOUKOVA, LAZAR LYUTAKOV	Both artists work with modular, mass-produced objects. Here, Rada Boukova used industrial synthetic building blocks, which she put together in a 'meaningful' way. Lazar Lyutakov created a sculpture series of acrylate glass, incorporating random fractures, and in addition supplemented this industrial glass substitute with real, handmade glass.
BURRI LA PITTURA, IRRIDUCIBILE PRESENZA	General Exhibition **10 MAY–28 JUL 2019** 10:00–18:00 daily **PAID ENTRY**	ALBERTO BURRI	A major retrospective of this pioneering 20th century Italian artist, renowned for his unorthadox collage materials and methods, such as tar, sand, plastics, and burning. Included around 50 works.
CANADA ISUMA	National Pavilion **11 MAY–24 NOV 2019** 10:00–18:00, closed Mon (except 13 May, 2 Sep, 18 Nov) **PAID ENTRY** **(BIENNALE TICKET)**	ISUMA (ZACHARIAS KUNUK, NORMAN COHN, PAUL APAK, PAULOOSIE QULITALIK)	Isuma – 'to think' in Inuktitut – is an Inuit artists' production group who preserve Inuit and other indigenous cultures via videos and online work. The films here covered forced resettlement in the 1950-60s, live webcasts from Nunavut around climate crisis, and the changes witnessed by a long-lived hunter.
CATALONIA IN VENICE_ TO LOSE YOUR HEAD (IDOLS)	Collateral Event **11 MAY–24 NOV 2019** 10:00–18:00, closed Mon	MARCEL BORRÀS WITH ALBERT GARCIA-ALZÓRRIZ AND THE COLLABORATION OF DAVID BESTUÉ, LUA CODERCH, LOLA LASURT, DANIELA ORTIZ, PEREJAUME, FRANCESC TORRES	Explored how statues can provoke physical reactions, both positive and negative. Included video, performance, an artist's book, and archives.
CHILE ALTERED VIEWS	National Pavilion **11 MAY–24 NOV 2019** 10:00–18:00 (10:00–20:00 Fri & Sat until 5 Oct), closed Mon (except 13 May, 2 Sep, 18 Nov) **PAID ENTRY** **(BIENNALE TICKET)**	VOLUSPA JARPA	A three-part archival show based on years of research, which aimed to subvert predominantly European, heterosexual, and male views of colonisation. Included the 'Hegemony Museum', examining six key historic moments; the 'Subaltern Portrait Gallery', six monumental oils; and film piece 'The Emancipating Opera', featuring a trans singer.
CHINA (PEOPLE'S REPUBLIC OF) RE-睿 / RE-RUI	National Pavilion **11 MAY–24 NOV 2019** 10:00–18:00 (10:00–20:00 Fri & Sat until 5 Oct), closed Mon (except 13 May, 2 Sep, 18 Nov) **PAID ENTRY** **(BIENNALE TICKET)**	CHEN QI, FEI JUN, HE XIANGYU, GENG XUE	Four artists from different generations gave their own take on 're', a common English prefix which in Mandarin sounds like 'rui', or 'wisdom'; the title thus means 'Re-wisdom'. This multi-media show – which had a layout based on classical Chinese gardens – aimed to be enjoyable, and emphasise similarities between today's China and the rest of the world.
CROATIA TRACES OF DISAPPEARING (IN THREE ACTS)	National Pavilion **11 MAY–24 NOV 2019** 10:00–18:00, closed Mon **FREE ENTRY**	IGOR GRUBIĆ	A humanist social documentary project, examining post-war Croatia's shift from socialism to capitalism. Three visually rich photo-essays or 'acts' covered changes in homes due to the privatisation of property; traditional vocations and crafts; and defunct post-industrial factories. An additional short film offered a social history of steel-working.

- - - - - KEY - - - - -

123 VENICE CITY MAP (P.8-11)   **A** ARSENALE MAP (P.12)   **G** GIARDINI MAP (P.13)

MAP KEY	ADDRESS	NOTES	TICK IF SEEN
15	Fondazione Ugo e Olga Levi Onlus, Palazzo Giustinian Lolin, San Marco 2893		◯
16	Fondazione Giorgio Cini Onlus, Isola di San Giorgio Maggiore		◯
G	Giardini		◯
17	Cantieri Navali (Shipyards), Fondamenta Quintavalle, San Pietro di Castello 40		◯
A	Arsenale		◯
A	Arsenale		◯
18	Calle della Regina (off Calle Corner, near the Prada Foundation), Santa Croce 2258		◯

CONTINUES OVER »

EXHIBITION CHECKLIST

ALL 90 NATIONAL PAVILIONS & 21 COLLATERAL EVENTS + 30 SELECTED EXHIBITIONS

PAVILION / EXHIBITION	DETAILS	ARTISTS	DESCRIPTION
CUBA ENTORNO ALECCIONADOR (A CAUTIONARY ENVIRONMENT)	NATIONAL PAVILION **11 MAY-24 NOV 2019** 11:00-16:00, closed Mon **FREE ENTRY**	ALEJANDRO CAMPINS, ALEX HÉRNANDEZ, ARIAMNA CONTINO & EUGENIO TIBALDI	Mixed-media group show on the relationship between humans and the environment. Included paintings of threatening bunkers; a huge paper-cut amidst 245 birch saplings, the paper's raw material; a project around bees in hives based on human cities; and symbolic sites of social idealism.
CYPRUS (REPUBLIC OF) UNTIMELY, AGAIN	NATIONAL PAVILION **11 MAY-24 NOV 2019** 10:00-18:00, closed Mon **FREE ENTRY**	CHRISTOFOROS SAVVA	Shortly before his untimely death, this pioneering Cypriot artist (1924-1968) was part of a group show representing the newly founded Republic of Cyprus at the 1968 Venice Biennale. Fifty years on, this survey – companion to a monograph – examined his crucial role in the island's art scene, and the many strands of his rich, referential practice.
CZECH + SLOVAK (REPUBLIC) (REPUBLIC) FORMER UNCERTAIN INDICATED	NATIONAL PAVILION **11 MAY-24 NOV 2019** 10:00-18:00, closed Mon (except 13 May, 2 Sep, 18 Nov) **PAID ENTRY** **(BIENNALE TICKET)**	STANISLAV KOLÍBAL	Since the early 1960s, this Czech artist has been exploring opposites such as stability/instability and certainty/uncertainty, with a conceptual, minimalist approach. Two new wall drawings (inside and outside) related to the modernist pavilion were presented with two earlier series: white sculptures from the 1960s, and wall installations from the 1970s.
DENMARK HEIRLOOM	NATIONAL PAVILION **11 MAY-24 NOV 2019** 10:00-18:00, closed Mon (except 13 May, 2 Sep, 18 Nov) **PAID ENTRY** **(BIENNALE TICKET)**	LARISSA SANSOUR	Danish-Palestinian Sansour draws inspiration from sci-fi, tackling themes of memory, history, and identity via imaginary future scenarios. This haunting film, set in Bethlehem decades after an eco-disaster, explored the very different reactions of two women tending a subterranean orchard. It was accompanied by a giant sphere that featured in the film.
DOMINICAN (REPUBLIC) NATURALEZA Y BIODIVERSIDAD EN LA REPÚBLICA DOMINICANA	NATIONAL PAVILION **11 MAY-24 NOV 2019** 10:00-18:00, closed Mon **FREE ENTRY**	DARIO OLEAGA, EZEQUIEL TAVERAS, HULDA GUZMÁN, JULIO VALDEZ, MIGUEL RAMIREZ, RITA BERTRECCHI, NICOLA PICA, MARRAFFA & CASCIOTTI	One of many presentations in this Biennale dealing with the global environmental crisis. The artists here aimed to take a positive stance, focusing on the dream-like beauty and mystery of their Caribbean island's luxuriant natural habitat.
DYSFUNCTIONAL	GENERAL EXHIBITION **8 MAY-24 NOV 2019** 10:00-18:00, closed Mon (last tickets 17:30) **PAID ENTRY**	ATELIER VAN LIESHOUT, VIRGIL ABLOH, MAARTEN BAAS, NACHO CARBONELL, WENDELL CASTLE, VINCENZO DE COTIIS, INGRID DONAT, STUDIO DRIFT, VINCENT DUBOURG, STUART HAYGARTH, STUDIO JOB, MATHIEU LEHANNEUR, FREDERIK MOLENSCHOT, RICK OWENS & MICHELE LAMY, RANDOM INTERNATIONAL, CHARLES TREVELYAN, VERHOEVEN TWINS	Site-specific works by a group of designer/makers from Carpenters Workshop Gallery, in dialogue with the venue's collection of Italian masters.
EGYPT KHNUM ACROSS TIMES WITNESS	NATIONAL PAVILION **11 MAY-24 NOV 2019** 10:00-18:00, closed Mon (except 13 May, 2 Sep, 18 Nov) **PAID ENTRY** **(BIENNALE TICKET)**	ISLAM ABDULLAH, AHMED CHIHA, AHMED ABDEL KARIM	Theme park-style installation emulating a futuristic Pharaonic tomb, including sphinxes with monitors and satellite dishes as heads, and named after Khnum, guardian of the temple's secrets. Was dogged by allegations of interference from the Egyptian government.

- - - - - KEY - - - - -

123 VENICE CITY MAP (P.8-11)   **A** ARSENALE MAP (P.12)   **G** GIARDINI MAP (P.13)

MAP KEY	ADDRESS	NOTES	TICK IF SEEN
13	Isola di San Servolo		◯
19	Associazione Culturale Spiazzi, Calle del Pestrin, Castello 3865		◯
G	Giardini		◯
G	Giardini		◯
20	Palazzo Albrizzi-Capello (Sala della Pace), Fondamenta Sant'Andrea, Cannaregio 4118		◯
21	Galleria Giorgio Franchetti alla Ca'd'Oro, Fondamenta Trapolin, Cannaregio 3932		◯
G	Giardini		◯

CONTINUES OVER ≫

Exhibition Checklist

ALL 90 NATIONAL PAVILIONS & 21 COLLATERAL EVENTS + 30 SELECTED EXHIBITIONS

PAVILION / EXHIBITION	DETAILS	ARTISTS	DESCRIPTION
EMILIO VEDOVA DI/BY GEORG BASELITZ	General Exhibition **18 APR-3 NOV 2019** 10:30-18:00, closed Mon, Tue **PAID ENTRY**	EMILIO VEDOVA	Two series of the Venetian painter's vast black-and-white canvases, selected and arranged by Georg Baselitz, who had his own exhibition up the road (see page 28 for details). It was housed in the Vedova Foundation's historic salt warehouse, beautifully updated by Italian starchitect Renzo Piano.
ESTONIA BIRTH V	National Pavilion **11 MAY-24 NOV 2019** 10:00-18:00, closed Mon **FREE ENTRY**	KRIS LEMSALU	Known for her works around the theme of death, the artist here — with a team of collaborators — celebrated the subject of birth and rebirth. Her fantastical immersive installation revelled in colourful, shamanic tableaux, including a multitude of legs and arms emerging from a column, and a blobby multi-limbed creature in a boat.
FINLAND (ALVAR AALTO PAVILION) A GREATER MIRACLE OF PERCEPTION	National Pavilion **11 MAY-24 NOV 2019** 10:00-18:00, closed Mon (except 13 May, 2 Sep, 18 Nov) **PAID ENTRY (BIENNALE TICKET)**	MIRACLE WORKERS COLLECTIVE (MARYAN ABDULKARIM, KHADAR AHMED, HASSAN BLASIM, GIOVANNA ESPOSITO YUSSIF, SONYA LINDFORS, BONAVENTURE SOH BEJENG NDIKUNG, OUTI PIESKI, LEENA PUKKI, LORENZO SANDOVAL, MARTTA TUOMAALA, CHRISTOPHER L. THOMAS, CHRISTOPHER WESSELS, SUVI WEST)	Collaborative event with talks, films, and a site-specific installation that reimagined the Alvar Aalto pavilion's ceiling as a garden. Part of a wider, multi-country project on transnationality and the traditional Sámi people who range across Norway, Sweden, Finland, and Russia.
FLAVIO FAVELLI: IL BELLO INVERSO	General Exhibition **9 MAY-15 SEP 2019** 10:30-18:00, closed Tue **PAID ENTRY**	FLAVIO FAVELLI	The theme of 'inverse beauty' informed this site-specific exhibition of 15 assemblages, arranged through the museum's grand rooms. Elements included wooden platforms from the Accademia Bridge, iron trellises, advertising signs, and other mementos of Venice life.
FÖRG IN VENICE	Collateral Event **11 MAY-23 AUG 2019** 10:00-18:00, closed Mon **FREE ENTRY**	GÜNTHER FÖRG	A survey of over 30 pieces from the late artist's varied oeuvre, concentrating on paintings and lesser-known sculptures. The intimate palazzo setting was intended to evoke an aura of romance and melancholy.
FRANCE DEEP SEE BLUE SURROUNDING YOU / VOIS CE BLEU PROFOND TE FONDRE	National Pavilion **11 MAY-24 NOV 2019** 10:00-18:00, closed Mon (except 13 May, 2 Sep, 18 Nov) **PAID ENTRY (BIENNALE TICKET)**	LAURE PROUVOST	Inspired by octopus tentacles, Prouvost transformed France's pavilion into a discombobulating labyrinth of dark and diaphanous sea-themed spaces, full of glass marine creatures and trash. Also included were a multilingual film of a journey from Paris to Venice, an entrance knocked into the basement, and — in a nod to Brexit — a 'tunnel' to the British pavilion next door.
FRANK AUERBACH: FROM PAINTING TO DRAWING	General Exhibition **1 MAY-3 AUG 2019** 10:00-13:00, 14:30-1900, closed Sun **FREE ENTRY**	FRANK AUERBACH	Commercial gallery show which included a major Auerbach oil painting never publicly displayed in Italy before. Auerbach's last Italian solo show was in 1986, when he represented Great Britain in the Venice Biennale, and won the prestigious Golden Lion prize.

- - - - - KEY - - - - -

123 VENICE CITY MAP (P.8-11)   A ARSENALE MAP (P.12)   G GIARDINI MAP (P.13)

MAP KEY	ADDRESS	NOTES	TICK IF SEEN
22	Fondazione Emilio e Annabianca Vedova, Fondamenta Zattere ai Saloni, Dorsoduro 266		◯
23	c/o Legno & Legno, Giudecca 211		◯
G	Giardini		◯
24	Ca' Rezzonico, Fondamenta Rezzonico, Dorsoduro 3136		◯
25	Palazzo Contarini Polignac, Dorsoduro 874		◯
G	Giardini		◯
26	Alma Zevi, Salizzada San Samuele, San Marco 3357		◯

CONTINUES OVER »

EXHIBITION CHECKLIST

ALL 90 NATIONAL PAVILIONS & 21 COLLATERAL EVENTS + 30 SELECTED EXHIBITIONS

PAVILION / EXHIBITION	DETAILS	ARTISTS	DESCRIPTION
FUTURE GENERATION ART PRIZE 2019 @ VENICE	Collateral Event **11 MAY-18 AUG 2019** 10:00-18:00, closed Mon **FREE ENTRY**	EMILIJA ŠKARNULYTĖ, GABRIELLE GOLIATH, COOKING SECTIONS, MONIRA AL QADIRI, YU ARAKI, KORAKRIT ARUNANONDCHAI, KASPER BOSMANS, MADISON BYCROFT, ALIA FARID, RODRIGO HERNÁNDEZ, LAURA HUERTAS MILLÁN, MARGUERITE HUMEAU, ELI LUNDGAARD, TAUS MAKHACHEVA, TOYIN OJIH ODUTOLA, SONDRA PERRY, GALA PORRAS-KIM, JAKOB STEENSEN, DANIEL TURNER, ANNA ZVYAGINTSEVA, BASEL ABBAS AND RUANNE ABOU-RAHME	A very varied group show of prize-winners and nominees for this biannual prize for emerging artists, established by the Victor Pinchuk Foundation in 2009.
FUTUROMA	Collateral Event **11 MAY-24 NOV 2019** 10:15-17:00, closed Mon **FREE ENTRY**	CELIA BAKER, JÁN BERKY, MARCUS-GUNNAR PETTERSSON, ÖDÖN GYÜGYI, BILLY KERRY, KLÁRA LAKATOS, DELAINE LE BAS, VALÉRIE LERAY, EMÍLIA RIGOVÁ, MARKÉTA ŠESTÁKOVÁ, SELMA SELMAN, DAN TURNER, ALFRED ULLRICH, LÁSZLÓ VARGA	Showcase for 14 Romani contemporary artists, aged between 27 and 95, from eight European countries.
GEORGIA REARMIRRORVIEW, SIMULATION IS SIMULATION, IS SIMULATION, IS SIMULATION	National Pavilion **11 MAY-24 NOV 2019** 10:00-18:00 (10:00-20:00 Fri & Sat until 5 Oct), closed Mon (except 13 May, 2 Sep, 18 Nov) **PAID ENTRY (BIENNALE TICKET)**	ANNA K.E.	A large-scale architectural environment of steel and coloured tiles conjured up a sleek, clinical bathroom, also referring to pixels at low resolution. Within it were video works referencing language and translation, and sculptures based on Asomtavruli – one of Georgia's three writing systems – spelling out the word 'deranged'.
GERMANY NATASCHA SÜDER HAPPELMANN	National Pavilion **11 MAY-24 NOV 2019** 10:00-18:00, closed Mon (except 13 May, 2 Sep, 18 Nov) **PAID ENTRY (BIENNALE TICKET)**	NATASCHA SÜDER HAPPELMANN	The pavilion was declared an immigration detention centre, with its grand portal barricaded, and a bleak interior of rocks, stained walls, and a shrill soundtrack based on migrants' whistles. The artist, born Natascha Sadr Haghighian, temporarily adopted this more German-sounding name, and wore a fake rock on her head for official events.
GHANA GHANA FREEDOM	National Pavilion **11 MAY-24 NOV 2019** 10:00-18:00 (10:00-20:00 Fri & Sat until 5 Oct), closed Mon (except 13 May, 2 Sep, 18 Nov) **PAID ENTRY (BIENNALE TICKET)**	FELICIA ABBAN, JOHN AKOMFRAH, EL ANATSUI, LYNETTE YIADOM BOAKYE, IBRAHIM MAHAMA, SELASI AWUSI SOSU	Ghana's inaugural pavilion, designed by Sir David Adjaye, boasted six strong artists from three generations. Included were Akomfrah's grand filmic meditations on colonisation; Yiadom-Boakye's fictional portraits of the African diaspora; Anatsui's shimmering bottle-top hangings; and 1960s images by Abban, Ghana's first professional female photographer.
GLASSTRESS 2019 (6TH EDITION)	General Exhibition **9 MAY-24 NOV 2019** 10:00-18:00, closed Wed **PAID ENTRY**	SAINT CLAIR CEMIN, PEDRO FRIEDEBERG, CARLOS GARAICOA, ARTUR LESCHER, PRUNE NOURRY, JOSÉ PARLA, PABLO REINOSO, VALESKA SOARES, TIM TATE, JANAINA TSCHÄPE, XAVIER VEILHAN, ROBERT WILSON, ROSE WYLIE, AI WEIWEI, MONICA BONVICINI, TONY CRAGG, SILRAZEH HOUSHIARY, KAREN LAMONTE, VIK MUNIZ, JAUME PLENSA, LAURE PROUVOST, THOMAS SCHÜTTE, SUDARSHAN SHETTY, KOEN VANMECHELEN, JOANA VASCONCELOS, ERWIN WURM, JEAN ARP, AYMAN BAALBAKI, MIROSLAW BALKA, ILONA BANNER, JAKE AND DINOS CHAPMAN, CESAR, MAT COLLISHAW, TRACEY EMIN, JAN FABRE, KENDELL GEERS, FRANCESCO CENNARI, ABDULNASSER GHAREM, MICHAEL JOO, ILYA & EMILIA KABAKOV, MICHAEL KIENZER, IM HEU LEE, OKSANA MAS, HANS OP DE BEEK, TONY OURSLER, JAVIER LEÓN PÉREZ, ANTONIO RIELLO, BERNARDÍ ROIG, JOYCE JANE SCOTT, WAEL SHAWKY, LINO TAGLIAPIETRA, FRED WILSON, DUSTIN YELLIN	Popular show of Murano glass works commissioned from a constellation of major artists, which returned for its sixth edition. This year it was displayed in an atmospheric ex-glass furnace on the island of Murano, still home to many traditional glass makers.
GREAT BRITAIN CATHY WILKES	National Pavilion **11 MAY-24 NOV 2019** 10:00-18:00, closed Mon (except 13 May, 2 Sep, 18 Nov) **PAID ENTRY (BIENNALE TICKET)**	CATHY WILKES	Natural light bathed this sparse, poetic installation in which a collection of small, homely treasures – rags, mannequins, plates, glassware – were assembled into mysterious scenes. From faceless, abject figures to pallid landscape paintings, the parade of melancholy, untitled objects conjured up a fragile domestic world long gone.

- - - - - KEY - - - - -

123 VENICE CITY MAP (P.8–11) **A** ARSENALE MAP (P.12) **G** GIARDINI MAP (P.13)

MAP KEY	ADDRESS	NOTES	TICK IF SEEN
27	IUAV University of Venice, Ca 'Tron, Santa Croce 1957		◯
28	Fondamenta Zattere allo Spitiro Santo, Dorsoduro 417		◯
A	Arsenale		◯
G	Giardini		◯
A	Arsenale		◯
29	Fondazione Berengo Art Space, Campiello della Pescheria, Murano		◯
G	Giardini		◯

CONTINUES OVER »

EXHIBITION CHECKLIST

ALL 90 NATIONAL PAVILIONS & 21 COLLATERAL EVENTS + 30 SELECTED EXHIBITIONS

PAVILION / EXHIBITION	DETAILS	ARTISTS	DESCRIPTION
GREECE MR STIGL	NATIONAL PAVILION **11 MAY-24 NOV 2019** 10:00-18:00, closed Mon (except 13 May, 2 Sep, 18 Nov) **PAID ENTRY** **(BIENNALE TICKET)**	PANOS CHARALAMBOUS, EVA STEFANI, ZAFOS XAGORARIS	Charalambous, who has collected sounds since the 1970s, provided a sonic carpet of 20,000 drinking glasses; Stefani's film documented marginal human stories, such as the everyday life of several middle-aged men; and Xagoraris recreated a prison gate built with forced labour in 1948, while the Greek pavilion displayed Peggy Guggenheim's art collection.
GRENADA EPIC MEMORY	NATIONAL PAVILION **11 MAY-24 NOV 2019** 10:00-18:00, closed Mon **FREE ENTRY**	AMY CANNESTRA, BILLY GERARD FRANK, DAVE LEWIS, SHERVONE NECKLES, FRANCO ROTA CANDIANI, ROBERTO MINIATI, CRS AVANT-GARDE	In this group of films and installations, Grenada's families became the subjects of history, including the found suitcases of a fisherman; the beautiful village of a 100-year-old father; and the grandmother who said 'tell your own story'. Meanwhile projections flashed in tiny jars, echoing the way local children catch fireflies.
GUATEMALA INTERESTING STATE	NATIONAL PAVILION **11 MAY-24 NOV 2019** 10:00-18:00, closed Mon **FREE ENTRY**	ELSIE WUNDERLICH, MARCO MANZO	In Guatemala, an 'interesting state' can mean pregnancy, but here referred to the country's record of violence against women, product of a machismo culture. Wunderlich's sculptures of women suffered signs of abuse, such as stitched-up mouths. Manzo presented a huge wall from which emerged male and female hands tattooed with macho symbols.
HAITI THE SPECTACLE OF TRAGEDY **(CANCELLED)**	NATIONAL PAVILION **7-11 MAY 2019** 10:00-18:00, closed Mon **FREE ENTRY**	JEAN ULRICK DÉSERT	Due to a lack of funding, the pavilion was cancelled at the last moment. The artist managed to present a few works in the Biennale's opening days, and the intended full show was listed in the Biennale catalogue. Works briefly shown included a nine-panel Caribbean map, a repainting of a Madrid beggar's sign, and drinks coasters with texts by Walter Benjamin.
HEARTBREAK	GENERAL EXHIBITION **11 MAY-24 NOV 2019** 10:00-18:00, closed Mon **FREE ENTRY**	MAJD ABDEL HAMID, TALAR AGHBASHIAN, LANA ČMAJČANIN, MARYAM HOSEINI, IMAD ISSA, FARAH KHELIL, RANDA MADDAH, FÜSUN ONUR, CHRISTIANA SOULOU	Explored the sadness felt by communities experiencing conflict, using the tale of Dido and Aeneas as a starting point. Sponsor Ruya Maps aims to support artists in areas of political and social instability.
HEIDI LAU: APPARITION	COLLATERAL EVENT **11 MAY-10 NOV 2019** 10:00-18:00, closed Mon **FREE ENTRY**	HEIDI LAU	Tactile, hand-built ceramic sculptural works explored themes of remembrance, also suggesting deconstructed items such as ritual objects, funeral monuments, and ancient fossils.
HILLARY: THE HILLARY CLINTON EMAILS	GENERAL EXHIBITION **9 MAY-24 NOV 2019** 08:00-21:30, closed Sun **FREE ENTRY**	KENNETH GOLDSMITH	You'd have needed a few weeks in order to read this: it featured all 60,000 of Hillary Clinton's leaked emails, as printed from the web by Goldsmith, a polemical artist/poet who works with big data. The installation incorporated replica Oval Office furnishings, and was housed in a former cinema.

- - - - - KEY - - - - -

(123) VENICE CITY MAP (P.8-11)　(A) ARSENALE MAP (P.12)　(G) GIARDINI MAP (P.13)

MAP KEY	ADDRESS	NOTES	TICK IF SEEN
G	Giardini		○
20	Palazzo Albrizzi-Capello (first floor), Fondamenta Sant'Andrea, Cannaregio 4118		○
20	Palazzo Albrizzi-Capello (first floor), Fondamenta Sant'Andrea, Cannaregio 4118		○
30	Circolo Ufficiali Marina (Navy Officers' Club), Fondamenta Arsenale, Castello 2168		○
31	Ca' del Duca, Corte del Duca Sforza, San Marco 3052		○
32	Campo della Tana, Castello 2126 / A		○
33	Despar Teatro Italia, Campiello de l'Anconeta, Cannaregio 1944		○

CONTINUES OVER »

Exhibition Checklist

ALL 90 NATIONAL PAVILIONS & 21 COLLATERAL EVENTS + 30 SELECTED EXHIBITIONS

PAVILION / EXHIBITION	DETAILS	ARTISTS	DESCRIPTION
HUNGARY IMAGINARY CAMERAS	NATIONAL PAVILION **11 MAY-24 NOV 2019** 10:00-18:00, closed Mon (except 13 May, 2 Sep, 18 Nov) **PAID ENTRY (BIENNALE TICKET)**	TAMÁS WALICZKY	Slick rendered images, created with newly developed design software, presented imaginary optical devices — cameras, projectors, and viewers — dreamed up by this new-media artist. He explored how the development of picture-recording devices has influenced our ways of looking at things — and how the attitudes of the devices' inventors influenced their machines.
ICELAND CHROMO SAPIENS	NATIONAL PAVILION **11 MAY-24 NOV 2019** 10:00-18:00, closed Mon **FREE ENTRY**	HRAFNHILDUR ARNARDÓTTIR / SHOPLIFTER	Hrafnhildur Arnardóttir, also known as Shoplifter, works entirely with synthetic hair. Here she created a womb-like cave environment, with hairy neon-hued stalactites hanging from the ceiling, and equally hirsute tussocks to rest on beneath. Three chambers led visitors from darkness to psychedelia to pastel hues — an immersive, selfie-friendly refuge from the outside world.
ICHICH – ICHIHR – ICHWIR / WE ALL HAVE TO DIE	COLLATERAL EVENT **8 MAY-24 NOV 2019** 10:00-18:00, closed Mon **PAID ENTRY**	JÖRG IMMENDORFF	The first major exhibition of the late German artist's work to be shown in an Italian institution. Focused on the self-referential aspect of his paintings, and his expressions of identity within them.
INDIA OUR TIME FOR A FUTURE CARING	NATIONAL PAVILION **11 MAY-24 NOV 2019** 10:00-18:00 (10:00-20:00 Fri & Sat until 5 Oct), closed Mon (except 13 May, 2 Sep, 18 Nov) **PAID ENTRY (BIENNALE TICKET)**	ATUL DODIYA, ASHIM PURKAYASTHA, GR IRANNA, JITISH KALLAT, NANDALAL BOSE, RUMMANA HUSSAIN, SHAKUNTALA KULKARNI	India's second-ever pavilion celebrated 150 years of Mahatma Gandhi. An inter-generational group of artists meditated on his ideas, with displays such as a wall of the humble wooden 'paduka' sandals Ghandi favoured, a misty video installation about his letter to Hitler urging peace, and nine glass-fronted cabinets from New Delhi's National Ghandi Museum, filled with haunting colonial-era curiosities.
INDONESIA LOST VERSES	NATIONAL PAVILION **11 MAY-24 NOV 2019** 10:00-18:00 (10:00-20:00 Fri & Sat until 5 Oct), closed Mon (except 13 May, 2 Sep, 18 Nov) **PAID ENTRY (BIENNALE TICKET)**	HANDIWIRMAN SAPUTRA & SYAGINI RATNA WULAN	Based on a proverb meaning roughly 'reason and negotiation never come just once', this was a gentle critique of Indonesia's fast-moving modern world. Beneath a huge wooden ferris wheel representing contemporary art's 'never-ending game' were scores of glass cabinets containing objects relating to Indonesia's history and culture, while on the ceiling flashed digital numbers — a reminder of passing time.
IRAN (ISLAMIC REPUBLIC OF) OF BEING AND SINGING	NATIONAL PAVILION **11 MAY-24 NOV 2019** 10:00-18:00, closed Mon **FREE ENTRY**	REZA LAVASSANI, SAMIRA ALIKHANZADEH, ALI MEER AZIMI	Intriguing group show inspired by a Iran's rich cultural heritage, and mounted amidst difficult US sanctions. Alikhanzadeh displayed wall-mounted images of women screened with mesh and poems, while Meer Azimi was inspired by French director Jean-Luc Godard. Central to it all was Lavassani's massive grey papier maché dining table, festooned with sculpted objects, that took four years to make.
IRAQ FATHERLAND	NATIONAL PAVILION **11 MAY-24 NOV 2019** 10:00-18:00, closed Mon **FREE ENTRY**	SERWAN BARAN	An installation of large site-specific sculptures and paintings evoking war zones and the world-view of a soldier, created by a Baghdad-born Kurd who has experienced over forty years of conflict, both as a soldier and a as war artist. The male-oriented title was a deliberate comment on the destructive paternalistic ideologies which continue to dominate this culture.

- - - - - KEY - - - - -

123 VENICE CITY MAP (P.8-11) **A** ARSENALE MAP (P.12) **G** GIARDINI MAP (P.13)

MAP KEY	ADDRESS	NOTES	TICK IF SEEN
G	Giardini		◯
34	Spazio Punch, Giudecca 800		◯
35	Fondazione Querini Stampalia, Campo Santa Maria Formosa, Castello 5252		◯
A	Arsenale		◯
A	Arsenale		◯
36	Fondaco Marcello, San Marco 3415		◯
31	Ca' del Duca, Corte del Duca Sforza, San Marco 3052		◯

CONTINUES OVER »

EXHIBITION CHECKLIST

ALL 90 NATIONAL PAVILIONS & 21 COLLATERAL EVENTS + 30 SELECTED EXHIBITIONS

PAVILION / EXHIBITION	DETAILS	ARTISTS	DESCRIPTION
IRELAND THE SHRINKING UNIVERSE	National Pavilion **11 MAY–24 NOV 2019** 10:00–18:00 (10:00–20:00 Fri & Sat until 5 Oct), closed Mon (except 13 May, 2 Sep, 18 Nov) **PAID ENTRY (BIENNALE TICKET)**	EVA ROTHSCHILD	An environment of large elements 'in conversation', with cloth-covered geometric forms, cardboard columns, and walls of ill-fitting concrete blocks echoing the Arsenale's dockyard feel. Scruffier and more colourful than the glossy S&M-tinged sculptures that made Rothschild's name, she described them as 'gone-wrong Ikea', and included seating for viewers.
ISRAEL FIELD HOSPITAL X	National Pavilion **11 MAY–24 NOV 2019** 10:00–18:00, closed Mon (except 13 May, 2 Sep, 18 Nov) **PAID ENTRY (BIENNALE TICKET)**	AYA BEN RON	Exploring the role of art amidst social ills, the pavilion was staged as a healthcare facility. The main event inside was the film 'No Body', based on the artist's personal experience of familial abuse. Visitors became patients, taking a queue number and choosing a 'Risk-Wristband'. Treatments included a 'Safe-Unit' and a 'Care-Chair'.
ITALY NEITHER NOR: THE CHALLENGE TO THE LABYRINTH	National Pavilion **11 MAY–24 NOV 2019** 10:00–18:00 (10:00–20:00 Fri & Sat until 5 Oct), closed Mon (except 13 May, 2 Sep, 18 Nov) **PAID ENTRY (BIENNALE TICKET)**	ENRICO DAVID, LILIANA MORO, CHIARA FUMAI	Named after a seminal 1962 essay by author Italo Calvino, this celebration of three major Italian artists included historic and never-before seen works. High white walls with various cut-outs divided Italy's huge warehouse into into a series of clinical architectural spaces for the artists' varied and unsettling installations, while an open-ended exhibition route allowed multiple readings.
IVORY COAST THE OPEN SHADOWS OF MEMORY	National Pavilion **11 MAY–24 NOV 2019** 10:00–18:00, closed Mon **FREE ENTRY**	ERNEST DÜKÜ, ANANIAS LEKI DAGO, VALÉRIE OKA, TONG YANRUNAN	A group show around identity and history. Dükü's dense assemblages employed folk symbols such as the spider, clearly prefiguring African diaspora traditions like Voodoo and Carnival; Dago showed lyrical black-and-white street photos of Ivory Coast's younger generations; Oka's painterly photo-collages referenced history and heroes; and Yanrunan painted dark portraits with unsettling, brushy features.
JANNIS KOUNELLIS	General Exhibition **MAY 11–NOV 24 2019** 10:00–18:00, closed Tue **PAID ENTRY**	JANNIS KOUNELLIS	Curated by Arte Povera expert Germano Celant, this was a huge retrospective of the pioneering Greek conceptualist, who died in 2017. Included around 70 works, tracing his career from 1958 to 2016.
JAPAN COSMO-EGGS	National Pavilion **11 MAY–24 NOV 2019** 10:00–18:00, closed Mon (except 13 May, 2 Sep, 18 Nov) **PAID ENTRY (BIENNALE TICKET)**	MOTOYUKI SHITAMICHI, TARO YASUNO, TOSHIAKI ISHIKURA, FUMINORI NOUSAKU	Well-integrated collaboration between artist Shitamichi, composer Yasuno, anthropologist Ishikura, and architect Nousaku. Visitors sat on a huge squishy cushion which seemed to 'breathe' while it powered the ghostly, bird-like music of automated wind instruments nearby. Huge, contemplative videos of 'tsunami boulders' washed up from the ocean surrounded the seating.
JEAN DUBUFFET AND VENICE	General Exhibition **10 MAY–20 OCT 2019** 10:00–18:00, closed Mon **PAID ENTRY**	JEAN DUBUFFET	Focused on the relationship that Art Brut ('raw art') inventor Dubuffet had with city of Venice, where he twice debuted works. Featured three major series: 'Célébration du Sol', 'Hourloupe', and 'Mires'.

- - - - - KEY - - - - -

123 VENICE CITY MAP (P.8-11)   A ARSENALE MAP (P.12)   G GIARDINI MAP (P.13)

MAP KEY	ADDRESS	NOTES	TICK IF SEEN
A	Arsenale		◯
G	Giardini		◯
A	Arsenale		◯
37	Castello Gallery, Riva dei Sette Martiri, Castello 1636/A		◯
38	Fondazione Prada, Ca' Corner della Regina, Calle Corner, Santa Croce 2215		◯
G	Giardini		◯
39	ACP Palazzo Franchetti, San Marco 2847		◯

CONTINUES OVER »

EXHIBITION CHECKLIST

ALL 90 NATIONAL PAVILIONS & 21 COLLATERAL EVENTS + 30 SELECTED EXHIBITIONS

PAVILION / EXHIBITION	DETAILS	ARTISTS	DESCRIPTION
JOAN JONAS: MOVING OFF THE LAND II	**General Exhibition** **24 MAR-29 SEP 2019** 11:00-19:00, closed Mon **FREE ENTRY**	**JOAN JONAS**	A major new project by this pioneering video and performance artist, examining the biodiversity of the seas. It launched the venue Ocean Space, in the newly restored Church of San Lorenzo (which used to be known for sheltering the city's stray cats).
KIRIBATI PACIFIC TIME – TIME FLIES	**National Pavilion** **11 MAY-24 NOV 2019** 10:00-18:00, closed Mon **FREE ENTRY**	KAEKA MICHAEL BETERO, DANIELA DANICA TEPES, KAIRAKEN BETIO GROUP; TEROLOANG BORDUEA, NENEIA TAKOIKOI, TINETA TIMIRAU, TEET AALOA, KENNETH IOANE, KAUMAI KAOMA, RUNETA KABWAA, OBETA TAIA, TIRIBO KOBAUA, TAMUERA TEBEBE, KAERAUEA RUE, TEUEA KABUNARE, TOKINTEKAI EKENTETAKE, KATANUTI FRANCIS, MIKAERE TEBWEBWE, TERETA ETINIKARAWA, KAELIA KOBAUA, RAATU TIUTEKE, KAERITI BAANGA, IOANNA FRANCIS, TEMARERE BANAAN, AANAMARIA TOOM, EINAKO TEMEWI, NIMEI ETINIKARAWA, TENITEITI MIKAERE, AANIBO BWATANITA, ARIN TIKIRAUA	Interlinked multi-genre artworks by 29 artists from different generations. All expressed their passion for this fragile atoll nation, increasingly threatened by flooding and climate change.
KOREA (REPUBLIC OF) HISTORY HAS FAILED US, BUT NO MATTER	**National Pavilion** **11 MAY-24 NOV 2019** 10:00-18:00, closed Mon (except 13 May, 2 Sep, 18 Nov) **PAID ENTRY (BIENNALE TICKET)**	**HWAYEON NAM, SIREN EUN YOUNG JUNG, JANE JIN KAISEN**	Three female artists exploring gender issues. Jung documented Yeoseong Gukgeuk, a waning genre of women-only theatre. Kaisen interpreted the Bari myth, about a daughter shunned by her community. Nam celebrated pioneering choreographer Choi Seung-hee, who defected to North Korea. The show's title references Min Jin Lee's novel 'Pachinko', which examines Korean society, and women's subordinate role within it.
KOSOVO (REPUBLIC OF) FAMILY ALBUM	**National Pavilion** **11 MAY-24 NOV 2019** 10:00-18:00 (10:00-20:00 Fri & Sat until 5 Oct), closed Mon (except 13 May, 2 Sep, 18 Nov) **PAID ENTRY (BIENNALE TICKET)**	**ALBAN MUJA**	A video installation investigating how media has shaped personal memories of Europe's last 20th-century war, the Kosovo conflict of 1998-1999. The Pristina-based artist tracked down four young adults who had been pictured in photojournalists' shots of child refugees – thus disseminating their traumatic experiences around the world – and sought their current reactions to the images.
LATVIA SAULES SUNS	**National Pavilion** **11 MAY-24 NOV 2019** 10:00-18:00 (10:00-20:00 Fri & Sat until 5 Oct), closed Mon (except 13 May, 2 Sep, 18 Nov) **PAID ENTRY (BIENNALE TICKET)**	**DAIGA GRANTIŅA**	A play on the phenomenon of 'sun-dogs' – an illusion whereby luminous patches appear either side of the sun – and ideas of decentralisation. Colourful, fragile-looking spiral assemblages of wire and fabric hung from the roof against a clean white room, suggesting a weird landscape garden, and referencing the disembodied experience of online worlds.
LETIZIA BATTAGLIA: PHOTOGRAPHY AS A LIFE CHOICE	**General Exhibition** **20 MAR-18 AUG 2019** 10:00-19:00, closed Tue **PAID ENTRY**	**LETIZIA BATTAGLIA**	Major survey of this Sicilian photographer, who explores social and political themes. Included over 300 of her works, many never shown before. Housed in a striking Giudecca landmark, the neo-Gothic 'house of three eyes'. Further photographic exhibitions were due to follow.
LITHUANIA SUN & SEA (MARINA)	**National Pavilion** **11 MAY-31 OCT 2019** 10:00-18:00, closed Mon Performances: Sat only, 10:00-18:00 **FREE ENTRY**	**LINA LAPELYTE, VAIVA GRAINYTE & RUGILE BARZDZIUKAITE**	The audience watched, from a mezzanine above, an opera-performance set on a busy sandy beach recreated in a raw industrial space. Below them, 'sunbathing' performers – adults and children of all ages – sang songs of everyday life, revealing their personalities and stories, plus some anxiety around climate crisis. The hit of the Biennale, with massive queues, and the Golden Lion for best national participation.

123 VENICE CITY MAP (P.8-11) **A** ARSENALE MAP (P.12) **G** GIARDINI MAP (P.13)

MAP KEY	ADDRESS	NOTES	TICK IF SEEN
40	Chiesa di San Lorenzo, Campo San Lorenzo, Castello		◯
41	European Cultural Centre, Palazzo Mora, Strada Nova, Cannaregio 3659		◯
G	Giardini		◯
A	Arsenale		◯
A	Arsenale		◯
42	Casa dei Tre Oci, Fondamenta delle Zitelle, Giudecca 43		◯
43	Marina Militare, Calle de la Celestia (in a gated military complex off Campo de la Celestia), Castello 2738c		◯

CONTINUES OVER »

Exhibition Checklist

ALL 90 NATIONAL PAVILIONS & 21 COLLATERAL EVENTS + 30 SELECTED EXHIBITIONS

PAVILION / EXHIBITION	DETAILS	ARTISTS	DESCRIPTION
LIVING ROCKS: A FRAGMENT OF THE UNIVERSE	COLLATERAL EVENT **8 MAY-24 NOV 2019** 10:00-18:00, closed Mon **FREE ENTRY**	JAMES DARLING, LESLEY FORWOOD	Sculpture, moving image, and sound combined in this historic salt warehouse to recreate a pool of rock-like 'thrombolites'. For three billion years such objects were the only living things on earth, and they helped to create our planet's atmosphere.
LORE BERT: ILLUMINATION. WAYS TO EUREKA	GENERAL EXHIBITION **7 MAY-24 NOV 2019** 10:00-18:00, closed Mon (times may vary) **FREE ENTRY**	LORE BERT	Two rainbow-hued towers of light-refractive glass rose above a sea of crumpled white papers in this historic church, where Casanova was baptised. It is also home to some wonderful 1490s frescos, which were restored in 2000.
LUC TUYMANS: LA PELLE	GENERAL EXHIBITION **24 MAR 2019-1 JUN 2020** 10:00-19:00, closed Mon **PAID ENTRY**	LUC TUYMANS	The first Italian solo exhibition by this influential Belgian figurative (and history) painter, with over 80 of his works plus a new site-specific piece. The show's overall theme referenced Curzio Malaparte's 1949 novel 'La Pelle' ('The Skin').
LUIGI PERICLE (1916–2001). BEYOND THE VISIBLE	GENERAL EXHIBITION **11 MAY-24 NOV 2019** 10:00-18:00, closed Mon **PAID ENTRY**	LUIGI PERICLE	A retrospective of this counter-cultural artist and scholar, who was influenced by esoteric doctrines such as theosophy. After his death in 2001, his home was not opened for 15 years, whereupon it revealed a vast haul of his art and writings — some of which were on display here.
LUOGO E SEGNI (PLACE AND SIGNS)	GENERAL EXHIBITION **24 MARCH-15 DEC 2019** 10:00-19:00, closed Mon **PAID ENTRY**	ETEL ADNAN, BERENICE ABBOTT, GIOVANNI ANSELMO, LUCAS ARRUDA, HICHAM BERRADA, LOUISE BOURGEOIS, CHARBEL-JOSEPH H. BOUTROS, CONSTANTIN BRANCUSI, NINA CANELL, VIJA CELMINS, TACITA DEAN, EDITH DEKYNDT, LIZ DESCHENES, TRISHA DONNELLY, SIMONE FATTAL, DOMINIQUE GONZÁLEZ-FOERSTER, FÉLIX GONZÁLEZ-TORRES, RONI HORN, ANN VERONICA JANSSENS, LEE LOZANO, AGNES MARTIN, JULIE MEHRETU, AKI BENJAMIN MEYERS, PHILIPPE PARRENO, ALESSANDRO PIANGIAMORE, R. H. QUAYTMAN, CAROL RAMA, LALA RUKH, STEPHANIE SAADE, ANRI SALA, RUDOLF STINGEL, STURTEVANT, TATIANA TROUVE, WU TSANG, ROBERT WILSON, CERITH WYN EVANS	Show named after a Carol Rama painting, with 100 works by 36 artists, in the Pinault collection's grand old customs house venue.
LUXEMBOURG (GRAND DUCHY OF) WRITTEN BY WATER	NATIONAL PAVILION **11 MAY-24 NOV 2019** 10:00-18:00 (10:00-20:00 Fri & Sat until 5 Oct), closed Mon (except 13 May, 2 Sep, 18 Nov) **PAID ENTRY (BIENNALE TICKET)**	MARCO GODINHO	A poignant 'library' of the artist's travel notebooks, water-bleached in the sea, and laid up a ramp as if on a wave. Behind was a video documenting his actions, plus meetings with migrants and blind people responding to his books and the sea. The work drew upon Portuguese-born Godinho's view of Luxembourg as a migrant-based land-locked island, and the Mediterranean as a huge cemetery.
MADAGASCAR I HAVE FORGOTTEN THE NIGHT	NATIONAL PAVILION **11 MAY-24 NOV 2019** 10:00-18:00 (10:00-20:00 Fri & Sat until 5 Oct), closed Mon (except 13 May, 2 Sep, 18 Nov) **PAID ENTRY (BIENNALE TICKET)**	JOËL ANDRIANOMEARISOA	Madagascar's inaugural pavilion aimed to be free from clichés of African exoticism. An immersive dark labyrinth of black tissue paper invited viewers to explore its apertures and textures and get lost in the cavern, as if touching the night. Invoked the fragility and intensity of darkness, plus ideas of duality, taboo, double entrance, lost memories, and identity.

- - - - - KEY - - - - -

123 VENICE CITY MAP (P.8-11)   **A** ARSENALE MAP (P.12)   **G** GIARDINI MAP (P.13)

MAP KEY	ADDRESS	NOTES	TICK IF SEEN
44	Magazzino del Sale No. 5, Fondamenta Zattere ai Saloni, Dorsoduro 262		○
45	Chiesa di San Samuele, Campo San Samuele, San Marco 5226B		○
46	Palazzo Grassi, Campo San Samuele, San Marco 3231		○
35	Fondazione Querini Stampalia, Campo Santa Maria Formosa, Castello 5252		○
47	Punta della Dogana, Dorsoduro 2		○
A	Arsenale		○
A	Arsenale		○

CONTINUES OVER »

EXHIBITION CHECKLIST

ALL 90 NATIONAL PAVILIONS & 21 COLLATERAL EVENTS + 30 SELECTED EXHIBITIONS

» MALAYSIA TO MONTENEGRO

PAVILION / EXHIBITION	DETAILS	ARTISTS	DESCRIPTION
MALAYSIA HOLDING UP A MIRROR	NATIONAL PAVILION **11 MAY-24 NOV 2019** 10:00-18:00, closed Mon **FREE ENTRY**	ANURENDRA JEGADEVA, H.H.LIM, IVAN LAM, ZULKIFLI YUSOFF	This inaugural pavilion included only male artists, each using mass assemblages to riff on Malaysia's diverse cultures. Included Yusoff's 'garden' of fruity wooden objects; Lim's lyrical collection of humble, friendly chairs; Jegadeva's garish psychiatric ward of kitsch posters and furnishings; and Lam's barrage of TV screens, all facing the wall, simultaneously playing Malaysian films of the 1960s onwards.
MALTA MALETH / HAVEN / PORT – HETEROTOPIAS OF EVOCATION	NATIONAL PAVILION **11 MAY-24 NOV 2019** 10:00-18:00 (10:00-20:00 Fri & Sat until 5 Oct), closed Mon (except 13 May, 2 Sep, 18 Nov) **PAID ENTRY (BIENNALE TICKET)**	VINCE BRIFFA, KLITSA ANTONIOU, TREVOR BORG	A group of Mediterranean-themed installations around the idea of Maleth, Phoenician for haven. Inspired by 'The Odyssey', Briffa's films explored the idea of safety. Borg's site-specific work navigated through the prehistoric layers of Malta. Antoniou investigated Atlantropa, a 1920s proposal to drain the Mediterranean and form a European supercontinent, by German architect Herman Sörgel.
MAY YOU LIVE IN INTERESTING TIMES	MAIN BIENNALE SHOW **11 MAY-24 NOV 2019** 10:00-18:00 (Arsenale 10:00-20:00 Fri & Sat until 5 Oct), closed Mon (except 13 May, 2 Sep, 18 Nov) **PAID ENTRY (BIENNALE TICKET)**	SEE PAGES 64–67 FOR DETAILS OF ARTISTS	The massive two-site title exhibition of the Biennale. See the next section for full details of all artists.
MEETINGS ON ART	PERFORMANCE PROGRAMME **8-12 MAY, 14 JUN, 14-15 SEP, 22 OCT, 23-24 NOV 2019** Various times **FREE ENTRY IN PUBLIC AREAS**	ALEX BACZYNSKI-JENKINS, ANGELA VETTESE, ANICKA YI, BO ZHENG, BOYCHILD, COOKING SECTIONS, DOMINIQUE GONZALEZ-FOERSTER, EVE STAINTON, FLORENCE PEAKE, INVERNOMUTO, LARA FAVARETTO, MARGARET WERTHEIM, MARYSIA LEWANDOWSKA, NASTIO MOSQUITO, NKISI, PAOLO BARATTA, PAUL MAHEKE, RALPH RUGOFF, TOMÁS SARACENO, VICTORIA SIN, VIVIAN CACCURI, VIVIEN SANSOUR, ZADIE XA	The official performance strand of the Biennale.
MEXICO ACTOS DE DIOS / ACTS OF GOD	NATIONAL PAVILION **11 MAY-24 NOV 2019** 10:00-18:00 (10:00-20:00 Fri & Sat until 5 Oct), closed Mon (except 13 May, 2 Sep, 18 Nov) **PAID ENTRY (BIENNALE TICKET)**	PABLO VARGAS LUGO	Stories from the Bible were used to parallel prophecy, fulfilment, and scripture with screenplay, filming, and editing – the modern narration form. Two films questioned ideas of the gospel as a perfect text, with unfinished scenes and takes where things go wrong. It posited a doubting figure of Jesus who does not want to fulfil his mission, because he doesn't know what he should be saving us from.
MONGOLIA A TEMPORALITY	NATIONAL PAVILION **11 MAY-24 NOV 2019** 10:00-18:00, closed Mon **FREE ENTRY**	JANTSANKHOROL ERDENEBAYAR WITH THE PARTICIPATION OF TRADITIONAL MONGOLIAN THROAT SINGERS AND CARSTEN NICOLAI (ALVA NOTO)	Evoked the traditions of a once-nomadic people who, by moving to the city, have been losing their connection to nature. Jantsa's disorienting red-lit installation suggested a dystopian wood, while all around echoed Nicolai's haunting soundtrack, which combined the ancient shamanistic practice of Mongolian throat-singing with electronic sounds and production.
MONTENEGRO ODISEJA / AN ODYSSEY	NATIONAL PAVILION **11 MAY-24 NOV 2019** 10:00-18:00, closed Mon **FREE ENTRY**	VESKO GAGOVIĆ	Inspired by Stanley Kubrick's '2001: a Space Odyssey', themes included alien life, science as religion, and humans' impact on the planet. Three geometric monoliths hovered, beaming white light from within; their metallic coats of gold, silver, and black represented sun, moon, and earth. Although each element – including the related wall works – could be considered separately, together they formed a whole.

- - - - - KEY - - - - -

(123) VENICE CITY MAP (P.8-11)   (A) ARSENALE MAP (P.12)   (G) GIARDINI MAP (P.13)

MAP KEY	ADDRESS	NOTES	TICK IF SEEN
48	Palazzo Malipiero, Ramo Malipiero, San Marco 3198		◯
A	Arsenale		◯
A / G	(A) Arsenale / (G) Giardini (Central Pavilion)		◯ ◯
49	Teatro Piccolo, Campo della Tana, Castello 2169/F, and around Giardini / Arsenale		◯
A	Arsenale		◯
50	Bruchium Fermentum, Calle del Forno (off Fondamenta de la Tana), Castello 2093-2090		◯
48	Palazzo Malipiero (piano terra), Ramo Malipiero, San Marco 3078-3079/A		◯

CONTINUES OVER »

EXHIBITION CHECKLIST

ALL 90 NATIONAL PAVILIONS & 21 COLLATERAL EVENTS + 30 SELECTED EXHIBITIONS

» MOZAMBIQUE TO PAKISTAN

PAVILION / EXHIBITION	DETAILS	ARTISTS	DESCRIPTION
MOZAMBIQUE (REPUBLIC OF) THE PAST, THE PRESENT AND THE IN BETWEEN	National Pavilion **11 MAY-24 NOV 2019** 10:00-18:00, closed Tue **FREE ENTRY**	GONÇALO MABUNDA, MAURO PINTO, FILIPE BRANQUINHO	Examined Mozambique's troubled past, with three artists who grew up during its bloody post-colonial civil war of 1977-1992, following the 1975 independence from Portugal. Anti-war activist Mabunda is renowned for anthropomorphic sculptures made from weapons; Branquinho showed photo-collages of authority figures in traditional masks; and Pinto's large-scale photo series 'Black Money' documented mine workers in tough conditions.
NETHERLANDS (THE) THE MEASUREMENT OF PRESENCE	National Pavilion **11 MAY-24 NOV 2019** 10:00-18:00, closed Mon (except 13 May, 2 Sep, 18 Nov) **PAID ENTRY (BIENNALE TICKET)**	IRIS KENSMIL, REMY JUNGERMAN	Two artists linked by questioning the heritage of modernism. Kensmil researched black female utopians to create seven portrait paintings, set on a faux-constructivist mural. Jungerman's Mondrianesque constructions – hanging 'ships' and a giant table standing in cracked mud – combined traditional pan-African motifs with 20th-century modernism, to trace the former's influence on the latter.
NEW ZEALAND POST HOC	National Pavilion **11 MAY-24 NOV 2019** 10:00-18:00, closed Mon **FREE ENTRY**	DANE MITCHELL	Over 260 lists of defunct phenomena, such as former nations and lost films, spooled out of a printing machine, and were read from an echo-free chamber. Phone masts disguised as pine trees relayed them in four public locations: outside IUAV architecture faculty; in the Ospedale (hospital) courtyard; in Parco Rimembranze Sant'Elena gardens; and a garden at Arsenale Nord.
NORDIC COUNTRIES (FINLAND, NORWAY, SWEDEN) WEATHER REPORT: FORECASTING FUTURE	National Pavilion **11 MAY-24 NOV 2019** 10:00-18:00, closed Mon (except 13 May, 2 Sep, 18 Nov) **PAID ENTRY (BIENNALE TICKET)**	ANE GRAFF, INGELA IHRMAN, NABBTEERI	Projects on nature and climate change, set in the apposite surrounds of a pavilion with trees inside. Collective nabbteeri used Giardini compost to create a self-maintaining ecosystem. Graff's glass cabinets suggested an inflamed body, with active ingredients evolving new mixtures. Ihrman's performance-oriented installation related sea organisms – such as seaweed, algae, and coral – to humanity's liquid origins.
NORTH MACEDONIA (REPUBLIC OF) SUBVERSION TO RED	National Pavilion **11 MAY-24 NOV 2019** 10:00-18:00, closed Mon **FREE ENTRY**	NADA PRLJA	Revisited theories of Marxism and Modernism in an attempt to reclaim socialism from nostalgia, and reacquaint today's society with 'forgotten' idealistic concepts such as 'solidarity'. The multi-disciplinary show included performance-based debates between contemporary thinkers and curators, and installations of socialist-era art, with 1960s Yugoslavian works from the collection of MoCA Skopje.
PABLO BRONSTEIN: CAROUSEL	General Exhibition **07 MAY-24 NOV 2019** 10:00-18:00, closed Mon **FREE ENTRY**	PABLO BRONSTEIN	This grand music room hosted a video of a performance piece inspired by the 19th century zootrope – a mechanical carousel which rotates, creating the illusion of moving images, and prefiguring contemporary screen culture.
PAKISTAN MANORA FIELD NOTES	National Pavilion **11 MAY-24 NOV 2019** 10:00-18:00, closed Mon **FREE ENTRY**	NAIZA KHAN	Lyrical immersive show paying homage to Manora, a small island off Karachi, which the artist has mapped and explored for a decade. In a dark space gleamed brass recreations of second-hand trinkets from Karachi's bazaars, plus seven city maps inspired by old British weather charts of the area. A sound work and multi-screen video added further impressions of everyday life on this magical but little-celebrated shore.

- - - - - KEY - - - - -

123 VENICE CITY MAP (P.8–11) **A** ARSENALE MAP (P.12) **G** GIARDINI MAP (P.13)

MAP KEY	ADDRESS	NOTES	TICK IF SEEN
41	Palazzo Mora, Strada Nova, Cannaregio 3659		◯
G	Giardini		◯
51	Istituto di Scienze Marine, Palazzina Canonica, Riva Sette Martiri, Castello 1364 (main pavilion)		◯
G	Giardini		◯
52	Palazzo Rota Ivancich, Calle del Remedio, Castello 4421		◯
53	Salla della Musica, Complesso dell'Ospedaletto, Barbaria della Tole, Castello 6691		◯
54	Tanarte / Spazio Tana, Fondamenta de la Tana, Castello 2109/A & 2110-2111		◯

EXHIBITION CHECKLIST

ALL 90 NATIONAL PAVILIONS & 21 COLLATERAL EVENTS + 30 SELECTED EXHIBITIONS

PAVILION / EXHIBITION	DETAILS	ARTISTS	DESCRIPTION
PEGGY GUGGENHEIM: THE LAST DOGARESSA	General Exhibition **21 SEP 2019-27 JAN 2020** 10:00-18:00, closed Tue **PAID ENTRY**	SELECTED WORKS FROM THE PEGGY GUGGENHEIM COLLECTION	Traced Peggy Guggenheim's life as an art collector in Venice from 1948-1979. Included 20th century greats such as René Magritte, plus rarely seen works from lesser-known names including René Brô, Gwyther Irwin, Grace Hartigan, Kenzo Okada, and Tomonori Toyofuku.
PERU 'INDIOS ANTROPÓFAGOS' A BUTTERFLY GARDEN IN THE (URBAN) JUNGLE	National Pavilion **11 MAY-24 NOV 2019** 10:00-18:00 (10:00-20:00 Fri & Sat until 5 Oct), closed Mon (except 13 May, 2 Sep, 18 Nov) **PAID ENTRY (BIENNALE TICKET)**	CHRISTIAN BENDAYÁN, OTTO MICHAEL (1859-1934), MANUEL RODRÍGUEZ LIRA (1874-1933), SEGUNDO CANDIÑO RODRÍGUEZ, ANONYMOUS POPULAR ARTIFICER	A parallel between Europe's self-constructed vision of the Amazon, and transvestite aesthetics. Multimedia tableaux of glamorous revellers in indigenous and urban settings mixed Christian and pre-Columbian symbolism, united by a 'trans' butterfly emblem. Some images were tiled onto walls, referencing patterned *azulejos* imported from Europe.
PHILIPPE PARRENO	Collateral Event **11 MAY-24 NOV 2019** 10:00-19:30 Mon-Sat 10:30-19:30 Sun **FREE ENTRY**	PHILIPPE PARRENO	New installation continuing his work with micro-organisms. Enclosed in a chamber above this luxury goods shop, the viewer was immersed in a digitally controlled environment consisting of mirrors, louvres, sounds, air pulses, and fluctuating light that interacted with phosphorescent material on the walls.
PHILIPPINES ISLAND WEATHER	National Pavilion **11 MAY-24 NOV 2019** 10:00-18:00 (10:00-20:00 Fri & Sat until 5 Oct), closed Mon (except 13 May, 2 Sep, 18 Nov) **PAID ENTRY (BIENNALE TICKET)**	MARK O. JUSTINIANI	Truly immersive installation comprising three deep-looking wavy cylinders, like islands drifting on water. Each contained stacked vitrines relating to aspects of the archipelago's three major isles. Visitors could walk across their thick glass surfaces and peer down, giving the vertigo-inducing feeling of standing over bottomless archaeological digs. In fact the effect was created by mirrors, and the 'holes' were just two feet in depth.
PINO PASCALI. FROM IMAGE TO FORM	Collateral Event **11 MAY-24 NOV 2019** 10:00-18:00, closed Mon **FREE ENTRY**	PINO PASCALI	One of Italy's major practitioners of Pop Art and Arte Povera, Pascali died aged just 32, in a 1968 motorcycle accident. This new look at his work placed his sculptures and videos in context alongside his photographic research.
PITTURA/PANORAMA: PAINTINGS BY HELEN FRANKENTHALER, 1952–1992	General Exhibition **MAY 7–NOV 17 2019** 10:00-19:00, closed Mon **PAID ENTRY**	HELEN FRANKENTHALER	This American abstract expressionist's colour palette was informed by 1500s Venetian art, and was echoed by the sparse but evocative venue, one of Venice's cultural centres in Renaissance times. The show surveyed 14 of her paintings from 1952-1992, focusing on the relationship between the vertical and horizontal planes.
POLAND FLIGHT	National Pavilion **11 MAY-24 NOV 2019** 10:00-18:00, closed Mon (except 13 May, 2 Sep, 18 Nov) **PAID ENTRY (BIENNALE TICKET)**	ROMAN STAŃCZAK	One of the Biennale's show-stoppers, this was a real aircraft turned inside-out, so that it appeared to spew guts of metal — inversion being a strategy the artist has pursued since the 1990s. The vessel in question was a private plane typically used by world's rich elite, a commentary on both Poland's capitalist progress, and the wealth attracted by the Biennale.

- - - - - KEY - - - - -

123 VENICE CITY MAP (P.8-11)   **A** ARSENALE MAP (P.12)   **G** GIARDINI MAP (P.13)

MAP KEY	ADDRESS	NOTES	TICK IF SEEN
55	Peggy Guggenheim Collection, Palazzo Venier dei Leoni, Calle San Cristoforo, Dorsoduro 701		◯
A	Arsenale		◯
56	Espace Louis Vuitton Venice, Calle del Ridotto, San Marco 1353		◯
A	Arsenale		◯
57	Palazzo Cavanis, Fondamenta Zattere ai Gesuati, Dorsoduro 920		◯
58	Palazzo Grimani, Ramo Grimani, Castello 4858		◯
G	Giardini		◯

CONTINUES OVER »

Exhibition Checklist

ALL 90 NATIONAL PAVILIONS & 21 COLLATERAL EVENTS + 30 SELECTED EXHIBITIONS

PAVILION / EXHIBITION	DETAILS	ARTISTS	DESCRIPTION
PORTUGAL A SEAM, A SURFACE, A HINGE OR A KNOT	National Pavilion **11 MAY-24 NOV 2019** 10:00-18:00, closed Mon **FREE ENTRY**	LEONOR ANTUNES	A poetic installation of slim minimalistic wooden and glass forms in muted shades, transmuting the idea of everyday objects, such as lamps, into abstract sculptures. Inspired by Venetian cultural history, it referenced key architects and designers such as Carlo Scarpa. Parts were fabricated by traditional craftspeople, including one of the still-active carpentries that worked with Scarpa.
PROCESSIONAL: AN INSTALLATION BY TODD WILLIAMSON	Collateral Event **11 MAY-24 NOV 2019** 10:00-18:00, closed Mon **FREE ENTRY**	TODD WILLIAMSON	An installation to encourage contemplation, with large-scale canvases in an old vaulted passageway. The work included original writings, and a specially composed sound piece.
PSALM	General Exhibition **8 MAY-29 SEP 2019** 10:00-18:00, closed Sat (times may vary) **MUSEO EBRAICO: PAID ENTRY** **ATENEO VENETO: FREE ENTRY**	EDMUND DE WAAL	Two-part show by this renowned ceramicist and author. In the Jewish Ghetto's Canton Scuola synagogue (part of Museo Ebraico), works of porcelain, marble, and gold enlivened lesser-known spaces. In the Ateneo Veneto's Aula Magna room, an installation housed 2,000 translated books by exiled writers.
RENATA MORALES & MARINA ABRAMOVIĆ	General Exhibition **08 MAY-6 JUL 2019** 10:30-18:00, closed Tue **PAID ENTRY**	RENATA MORALES, MARINA ABRAMOVIĆ	Here, a mixed media installation by Mexican artist Morales met a virtual reality piece by performance pioneer Abramović. The former filled two halls with painted tyres, ceramic figures, and debris; the latter explored climate change by having her virtual image beckon from a tank of rising water.
ROMANIA UNFINISHED CONVERSATIONS ON THE WEIGHT OF ABSENCE	National Pavilion **11 MAY-24 NOV 2019** 10:00-18:00, closed Mon **GIARDINI: PAID ENTRY (BIENNALE TICKET)** **ISTITUTO ROMENO: FREE ENTRY**	BELU-SIMION FĂINARU, DAN MIHĂLȚIANU, MIKLÓS ONUCSÁN	The Giardini had recreations of important works by three artists from Romania's '1980s generation'. Onucsán showed a delicate white-on-white wall camouflage; Mihălțianu, a reflective black 'canal' on the floor, like an ominous oil slick; and Făinaru, a poignant 'memorial room' with banks of blank books. The pieces had changed over time, rejecting fixed histories. A further selection of work was at Istituto Romeno.
RUSSIA LC 15:11-32	National Pavilion **11 MAY-24 NOV 2019** 10:00-18:00, closed Mon (except 13 May, 2 Sep, 18 Nov) **PAID ENTRY (BIENNALE TICKET)**	ALEXANDER SOKUROV, ALEXANDER SHISHKIN-HOKUSAI	A melodramatic installation based on the Hermitage Museum's famous Rembrandt painting, 'The Return of the Prodigal Son'. It presented a hellish wooden mash-up of a Hermitage hall and a Flemish School artist's studio, filled with sinister automata, dark shadows, references to war and Christianity, and blood-red lighting. The title references the Gospel of Luke verses from which the parable originates.
SALON SUISSE: SLOW	Collateral Event **PROGRAMME EVENTS: 11 MAY; 19-21 SEP; 17-19 OCT; 21-23 NOV 2019** 10:00-18:00, closed Mon **FREE ENTRY**	ANJA RADOMIROVIC, BERTRAND GAUGUET, CAMILLE ABELE, CATHERINE CONTOUR, CÉLINE EIDENBENZ, CHARLOTTE LAUBARD, CHONJA LEE, CLEMENS KLOPFENSTEIN, EKLEKTO, ERIC PHILIPPOZ, GUIDO BONDOLF, HAMISH FULTON, HANS ULRICH OBRIST, HELEN HERSCH, ISABEL LEWIS, ISABELLE ALFONSI, JEREMIE GINDRE, KIMSOOJA, LAURENCE WAGNER, MAGALI LE MENS, MARIE VELARDI, MICHELE SAVORGNANO, NEVENA PULJIC, PAULINE BOUDRY, RAMIN & REDA, RENATE LORENZ, RICCARDO CALDURA, ROBIN MICHEL, SARA PAOLINI, SYLVAIN MENETREY, TOM HODGKINSON, TRISTAN WEDDIGEN, VICTORIA MÜHLIG, VIDYA GASTALDON, VINCENT BARRAS	A Swiss celebration of all things leisurely, with a participatory programme of events considering topics such as acceleration, bedding, slothing, and hypnosis.

- - - - - KEY - - - - -

(123) VENICE CITY MAP (P.8-11)   (A) ARSENALE MAP (P.12)   (G) GIARDINI MAP (P.13)

MAP KEY	ADDRESS	NOTES	TICK IF SEEN
(15)	Fondazione Ugo e Olga Levi Onlus, Palazzo Giustinian Lolin, San Marco 2893		◯
(4)	Santa Maria della Pietà, Riva degli Schiavoni, Castello 3701		◯
(59) (60)	(59) Museo Ebraico, Campo del Ghetto Nuovo, Cannaregio 2902/B (60) Ateneo Veneto, Campo San Fantin, San Marco 1897		◯ ◯
(24)	Ca' Rezzonico, Fondamenta Rezzonico, Dorsoduro 3136		◯
(G) (61)	(G) Giardini (61) Istituto Romeno, Palazzo Correr, Campo Santa Fosca, Cannaregio 2214		◯ ◯
(G)	Giardini		◯
(62)	Swiss Consulate, Palazzo Trevisan degli Ulivi, Campo Sant'Agnese, Dorsoduro 810		◯

CONTINUES OVER »

EXHIBITION CHECKLIST

ALL 90 NATIONAL PAVILIONS & 21 COLLATERAL EVENTS + 30 SELECTED EXHIBITIONS

》 SAN MARINO TO SHIRLEY TSE

PAVILION / EXHIBITION	DETAILS	ARTISTS	DESCRIPTION
SAN MARINO (REPUBLIC OF) FRIENDSHIP PROJECT INTERNATIONAL	National Pavilion **11 MAY-24 NOV 2019** 10:00-18:00, closed Mon **FREE ENTRY**	GISELLA BATTISTINI, MARTINA CONTI, GABRIELE GAMBUTI, GIOVANNA FRA, THEA TINI, CHEN CHENGWEI, LI GENG, DARIO ORTIZ, TANG SHUANGNING, JENS W. BEYRICH, XING JUNQIN, XU DE QI, SEBASTIAN	A varied selection of artists and work, presented by this tiny republic set within by Italy. Locals Battistini, Gambuti, and Tini were ahown alongside colleagues from South America, China, Italy, and Liechtenstein; genres included realism, pop art, abstraction, new media, and sculpture.
SAUDI ARABIA AFTER ILLUSION	National Pavilion **11 MAY-24 NOV 2019** 10:00-18:00 (10:00-20:00 Fri & Sat until 5 Oct), closed Mon (except 13 May, 2 Sep, 18 Nov) **PAID ENTRY (BIENNALE TICKET)**	ZAHRAH AL GHAMDI	Large internally-lit textiles were festooned with 52,000 shell-like boiled leather objects; squeezing them made a distinctive noise, relayed via a sound system. Everything was painstakingly hand-made by the artist, whose natural materials recall a childhood spent herding sheep with her grandfather. The title was inspired by an ancient Arabic poem about struggling to reconcile with home after a 20-year absence.
SCOTLAND + VENICE PRESENTS CHAASRLOTTE PRODGER SAF05	Collateral Event **11 MAY-24 NOV 2019** 10:00-18:00, closed Mon **FREE ENTRY**	CHARLOTTE PRODGER	The 2018 Turner Prize winner returned with a new single-channel video on the theme of 'queer wilderness', informed by her early years in rural Aberdeenshire. The film was inspired by her fascination with a gender-fluid lioness.
SEAN SCULLY: HUMAN	General Exhibition **11 MAY-13 OCT 2019** 10:00-18:00 Mon-Sat; 12:00-18:00 Sun **FREE ENTRY**	SEAN SCULLY	The 16th-century abbey and its vast manuscript collection inspired a series of varied works by this lyrical abstractionist, including stained glass windows and new figurative paintings. Scully's tallest-ever sculpture, a multicoloured felt column 10m high, soared beneath the central Palladian dome.
SERBIA REGAINING MEMORY LOSS	National Pavilion **11 MAY-24 NOV 2019** 10:00-18:00, closed Mon (except 13 May, 2 Sep, 18 Nov) **PAID ENTRY (BIENNALE TICKET)**	DJORDJE OZBOLT	A huge grey-toned landscape painting lined the pavilion walls, upon which were placed smaller, more colourful works depicting visionary retro-futurist scenes. Before them towered grey, blocky sculptures, melding fetish figure with brutalist architecture. A continuation of the artist's concern with the fragmentary nature of memory, and the socialist era.
SEYCHELLES (REPUBLIC OF) DRIFT	National Pavilion **11 MAY-24 NOV 2019** 10:00-18:00, closed Tue **FREE ENTRY**	GEORGE CAMILLE & DANIEL DODIN	Camille's bright environment of undulating white paper was embossed with motifs of plant, animal, and human forms, to evoke a tsunami of data. Dodin's crepuscular mutimedia installation celebrated Seychellois workers, especially the bottle collectors who recycle others' spent plastic. Recalling an archaeological dig, some darkened corners required a torch to examine.
SHIRLEY TSE: STAKEHOLDERS, HONG KONG IN VENICE	Collateral Event **11 MAY-24 NOV 2019** 10:00-18:00, closed Mon **FREE ENTRY**	SHIRLEY TSE	Craft and technology were combined in this sprawling installation of 3D-printed elements and hand-made wooden forms. An improvised sculptural 'badminton court' occupied the cloistered courtyard.

- - - - - KEY - - - - -

123 VENICE CITY MAP (P.8-11)   **A** ARSENALE MAP (P.12)   **G** GIARDINI MAP (P.13)

MAP KEY	ADDRESS	NOTES	TICK IF SEEN
53	**53** Complesso dell'Ospedaletto, Barbaria della Tole, Castello 6691		○
63	**63** Palazzo Bollani, Calle Bollani, Castello 3647		○
A	Arsenale		○
17	Arsenale Docks, Fondamenta Quintavalle, San Pietro di Castello 40		○
64	Abbazia di San Giorgio Maggiore, Isola di San Giorgio Maggiore		○
G	Giardini		○
41	Palazzo Mora, Strada Nova, Cannaregio 3659		○
32	Campo della Tana, Castello 2126		○

CONTINUES OVER »

Exhibition Checklist

ALL 90 NATIONAL PAVILIONS & 21 COLLATERAL EVENTS + 30 SELECTED EXHIBITIONS

PAVILION / EXHIBITION	DETAILS	ARTISTS	DESCRIPTION
SINGAPORE MUSIC FOR EVERYONE: VARIATIONS ON A THEME	NATIONAL PAVILION **11 MAY-24 NOV 2019** 10:00-18:00 (10:00-20:00 Fri & Sat until 5 Oct), closed Mon (except 13 May, 2 Sep, 18 Nov) **PAID ENTRY (BIENNALE TICKET)**	SONG-MING ANG	A video installation featuring 20 children performing, and improvising upon, the recorder – an instrument used to teach youngsters music in many countries. It referenced the Singapore government's idealistic 1970s 'Music for Everyone' series of public concerts, with displays of archive materials, sculptures of quirky reconfigured recorders, and playful assemblages of folded and cut sheet music.
SLOVENIA (REPUBLIC OF) HERE WE GO AGAIN ... SYSTEM 317	NATIONAL PAVILION **11 MAY-24 NOV 2019** 10:00-18:00 (10:00-20:00 Fri & Sat until 5 Oct), closed Mon (except 13 May, 2 Sep, 18 Nov) **PAID ENTRY (BIENNALE TICKET)**	MARKO PELJHAN	A literally futuristic work, by an artist who is also a board member of Slovenia's Space Science Centre. Here he presented a huge blue-lit neon and plexiglass model, representing a 'hypersonic vehicle' – one that travels much faster than sound, at Mach 5 and above. It was a comment on the global military industrial complex's current hypersonic arms race, but also on human possibilities and ambition.
SOUTH AFRICA (REPUBLIC OF) THE STRONGER WE BECOME	NATIONAL PAVILION **11 MAY-24 NOV 2019** 10:00-18:00 (10:00-20:00 Fri & Sat until 5 Oct), closed Mon (except 13 May, 2 Sep, 18 Nov) **PAID ENTRY (BIENNALE TICKET)**	DINEO SESHEE BOPAPE, TRACEY ROSE, MAWANDE KA ZENZILE	In the atmospheric renovated Sale d'Armi (Army Salt) warehouse, three artists presented a 'trialogue' on the resilience of South Africa's people. Ka Zenzile's images led the viewer in and out of Bopape's installation, while a voiceover from Rose's work linked the space. The title was inspired by the 1987 Labi Siffre song 'Something Inside So Strong', written in response to police violence during apartheid.
SPAIN PERFORATED	NATIONAL PAVILION **11 MAY-24 NOV 2019** 10:00-18:00, closed Mon (except 13 May, 2 Sep, 18 Nov) **PAID ENTRY (BIENNALE TICKET)**	ITZIAR OKARIZ, SERGIO PREGO	Two artists who explore alternative functions of body and space, in a show named after a Susan Sontag quote. Performance-based Okariz's videos included conversing with objects in museums, and 'yoga breathing' that sounded like the ocean. In the garden, Prego hung large 'pneumatic sculptures': bulging rubbery pouches, with water spilling from their lips.
SWITZERLAND MOVING BACKWARDS	NATIONAL PAVILION **11 MAY-24 NOV 2019** 10:00-18:00, closed Mon (except 13 May, 2 Sep, 18 Nov) **PAID ENTRY (BIENNALE TICKET)**	PAULINE BOUDRY / RENATE LORENZ	Inspired by Kurdish guerrilla women who wore shoes backwards to leave misleading traces in the snow, this film showed dancers experimenting with backwards movements. It was a comment on political and societal regression – the trend towards closed borders – but also suggested resistance. A joyous 'nightclub' sequence, with shimmering sparkly clothes, alluded to queer underground culture.
SYRIAN ARAB (REPUBLIC) SYRIAN CIVILIZATION IS STILL ALIVE	NATIONAL PAVILION **11 MAY-24 NOV 2019** 11:00-16:00, closed Mon **FREE ENTRY**	ABDALAH ABOUASSALI, GIACOMO BRAGLIA, IBRAHIM AL HAMID, CHEN HUASHA, SAED SALLOUM, XIE TIAN, SAAD YAGAN, PRIMO VANADIA, GIUSEPPE BIASIO	Syria played a crucial role in the foundation of both Christian and Islamic art, and has presented a Biennale pavilion since 2007, whatever the circumstances at home. The eclectic Syrian contributions here included Yagan's humanitarian paintings; Al Hamid, inspired by local traditions; Aboussali's realism; and Salloum's abstraction. The other artists were an international mix, ranging from China to Sicily.
THAILAND THE REVOLVING WORLD	NATIONAL PAVILION **11 MAY-24 NOV 2019** 10:00-18:00, closed Mon **FREE ENTRY**	SOMSAK CHOWTADAPONG, PANYA VIJINTHANASARN, KRIT NGAMSOM	Focused on stories and histories from different phases of the Thai Kingdom. Vijinthanasarn reinterpreted a Buddhist mural from the 1700s. Chowtadapong's lightbox paintings considered how tales grow wilder as they pass between generations. And Ngamsom created a glowing cabinet of Italo-Thai curiosities with a Ferris wheel at its centre, topped by a model of Bangkok railway station – designed by an Italian architect.

- - - - - KEY - - - - -

123 VENICE CITY MAP (P.8-11)   **A** ARSENALE MAP (P.12)   **G** GIARDINI MAP (P.13)

MAP KEY	ADDRESS	NOTES	TICK IF SEEN
A	Arsenale		◯
A	Arsenale		◯
A	Arsenale		◯
G	Giardini		◯
G	Giardini		◯
13	**13** Isola di San Servolo		◯
65	**65** Chiesetta della Misericordia, Campo dell'Abbazia, Cannaregio 3548-3549		◯
66	In Paradiso Art Gallery, Viale Trieste, Castello 1260		◯

CONTINUES OVER »

EXHIBITION CHECKLIST

ALL 90 NATIONAL PAVILIONS & 21 COLLATERAL EVENTS + 30 SELECTED EXHIBITIONS

PAVILION / EXHIBITION	DETAILS	ARTISTS	DESCRIPTION
THE DEATH OF JAMES LEE BYARS	Collateral Event **11 MAY-24 NOV 2019** 10:00-18:00, closed Mon **FREE ENTRY**	JAMES LEE BYARS, ZAD MOULTAKA	Recreation of Byars' famous 1994 installation, in which he donned a gold suit, lay down in a gold leaf-encrusted room, and 'vanished'. Moultaka created an immersive installation that responded to this.
THE NATURE OF ARP	General Exhibition **13 APR-2 SEP 2019** 10:00-18:00, closed Tue **PAID ENTRY**	JEAN (HANS) ARP	Wide-ranging survey of the 60-year career of this Franco-German surrealist sculptor and painter, who was a founder member of the Dada movement.
THE SPARK IS YOU: PARASOL UNIT IN VENICE	Collateral Event **9 MAY-23 NOV 2019** 10:00-18:00, closed Sun **FREE ENTRY**	MORTEZA AHMADVAND, NAZGOL ANSARINI, SIAH ARMAJANI, MITRA FARAHANI, SAHAND HESAMIYAN, Y.Z. KAM, FARIDEH LASHAI, KOUSHNA NAVABI, NAVID NUUR	A mixed exhibition of Iranian artists working across many genres, but all informed by a grounding in Persian poetry, and a desire to connect across cultures. Organised by London's Parasol Unit gallery.
THERE IS A BEGINNING AT THE END	General Exhibition **10 MAY-10 SEP 2019** 10:00-18:00, closed Mon **FREE ENTRY**	DMITRY KRYMOV, IRINA NAKHOVA, GARY HILL, !MEDIENGRUPPE BITNIK	To mark the 500th anniversary of the great Venetian painter Jacopo Tintoretto, each of the artists here rethought an aspect of his work.
TIME, FORWARD!	General Exhibition **11 MAY-20 OCT 2019** 12:00-20:00, closed Wed **FREE ENTRY**	ROSA BARBA, ALEKSANDRA DOMANOVIĆ, VALENTIN FETISOV, JOANA HADJITHOMAS AND KHALIL JOREIGE, DARIA IRINCHEEVA, ALEKSANDRA SUKHAREVA, CHRISTOPHER KULENDRAN THOMAS IN COLLABORATION WITH ANNIKA KUHLMANN, ADAM LINDER, HAROON MIRZA, TREVOR PAGLEN, WALID RAAD, JAMES RICHARDS, KIRILL SAVCHENKOV, WHERE DOGS RUN	13 new works about time, commissioned by Russian art foundation V-A-C, and titled after a 1930s Soviet novel.
TURKEY WE, ELSEWHERE	National Pavilion **11 MAY-24 NOV 2019** 10:00-18:00 (10:00-20:00 Fri & Sat until 5 Oct), closed Mon (except 13 May, 2 Sep, 18 Nov) **PAID ENTRY (BIENNALE TICKET)**	İNCİ EVINER	A disorienting sloped installation, with multiple levels and views of its blank grey walls, spiky furniture, metal grilles, and confusing stairways. Within it were projected deeply unsettling videos of anxious-looking people in disquieting, slowly unfolding scenarios. Add to this the weird sounds and lack of explanation other than 'collective displacement', and it was like a Kafka-meets-Escher nightmare of surveillance.
UKRAINE THE SHADOW OF DREAM CAST UPON GIARDINI DELLA BIENNALE	National Pavilion **11 MAY-24 NOV 2019** 10:00-18:00 (10:00-20:00 Fri & Sat until 5 Oct), closed Mon (except 13 May, 2 Sep, 18 Nov) **PAID ENTRY (BIENNALE TICKET)**	ALL ARTISTS OF UKRAINE	The world's largest cargo aircraft, the Ukrainian-built Antonov An-225 Mriya (meaning dream), was meant to fly over Venice on 9 May 2019, casting its shadow on the Giardini. Inside its hold would have been a hard drive, listing all the living artists of Ukraine who agreed to be included. Politics and practicalities meant it didn't happen; instead, the pavilion housed documentation of this bold project, and a banner listing the names.

- - - - - KEY - - - - -

123 VENICE CITY MAP (P.8-11) **A** ARSENALE MAP (P.12) **G** GIARDINI MAP (P.13)

MAP KEY	ADDRESS	NOTES	TICK IF SEEN
67	Chiesa di Santa Maria della Visitazione, Fondamenta Zattere ai Gesuati, Dorsoduro 919A		◯
55	Peggy Guggenheim Collection, Palazzo Venier dei Leoni, Calle San Cristoforo, Dorsoduro 701		◯
68	Benedetto Marcello Conservatory of Music in Venice, Campo Santo Stefano, San Marco 2810		◯
69	Chiesa di San Fantin, Campo San Fantin, San Marco 1390/a		◯
70	V-A-C Zattere, Palazzo della Zattere, Fondamenta Zattere al Ponte Longo, Dorsoduro 1401		◯
A	Arsenale		◯
A	Arsenale		◯

CONTINUES OVER »

EXHIBITION CHECKLIST

ALL 90 NATIONAL PAVILIONS & 21 COLLATERAL EVENTS + 30 SELECTED EXHIBITIONS

>> UNITED ARAB EMIRATES TO ZIMBABWE

PAVILION / EXHIBITION	DETAILS	ARTISTS	DESCRIPTION
UNITED ARAB EMIRATES PASSAGE	National Pavilion **11 MAY-24 NOV 2019** 10:00-18:00 (10:00-20:00 Fri & Sat until 5 Oct), closed Mon (except 13 May, 2 Sep, 18 Nov) **PAID ENTRY (BIENNALE TICKET)**	NUJOOM ALGHANEM	Video installation by a major poet, based on her 2009 poem 'The Passerby Collects the Moonlight'. Two sides of a huge screen told two stories, one fictional and one real, with the same soundtrack. The fiction followed a woman searching for home, losing her language on the way. The real version documented the fiction's making. Reflected the experience of Arab women – displaced or not – in a changing society.
UNITED STATES OF AMERICA LIBERTY	National Pavilion **11 MAY-24 NOV 2019** 10:00-18:00, closed Mon (except 13 May, 2 Sep, 18 Nov) **PAID ENTRY (BIENNALE TICKET)**	MARTIN PURYEAR	New work by a venerable artist – aged 77 in 2019 – who hand-crafts monumental sculptures with spare, allusive forms, using traditional materials such as wood, stone and metal. References abounded: a huge red Phrygian cap, Venetian fishermen's nets, Haitian slaves, civil war soldiers, Catholic symbolism, and artists such as Brancusi and Arp. The artist commented that he had 'tasted and spat out Minimalism'.
URUGUAY 'LA CASA EMPÁTICA'	National Pavilion **11 MAY-24 NOV 2019** 10:00-18:00, closed Mon (except 13 May, 2 Sep, 18 Nov) **PAID ENTRY (BIENNALE TICKET)**	YAMANDÚ CANOSA	Paintings, drawings, photographs, and murals considered the current obsession with borders. On the pavilion's facade, panels of grey, yellow, orange, and blue echoed the colours inside. Entered from the south, the space had been mapped as a 'total landscape', with South, East, North, and West walls reflecting their orientation in the Giardini. Completing it was the roof, a starry sky also reflected in the floor.
VENEZUELA (BOLIVARIAN REPUBLIC OF) METAPHOR OF THREE WINDOWS (VENEZUELA: IDENTITY IN TIME AND SPACE)	National Pavilion **19 MAY (OPENING WAS DELAYED)-24 NOV 2019** 10:00-18:00, closed Mon (except 13 May, 2 Sep, 18 Nov) **PAID ENTRY (BIENNALE TICKET)**	NATALIE ROCHA CAPIELLO, RICARDO GARCÍA, GABRIEL LÓPEZ, NELSON RANGELOSKY	The windows of Carlo Scarpa's stunning pavilion were used literally as a metaphor, striped with red film to give the interior a crimson glow. The work within had a shamanistic feel, with Garcia's huge charcoal heads of humans and birds; Rocha's bound textile hearts; Lopez's folkloric performances and masks; and Rangel's 3D screen of a lamenting woman's face morphing into that of Donald Trump. Opened a week late, and amidst protests, due to turmoil in Venezuela.
WALES IN VENICE: SEAN EDWARDS	Collateral Event **11 MAY-24 NOV 2019** 11:00-18:00, closed Mon **FREE ENTRY**	SEAN EDWARDS	This ex-convent was transformed by confessional sculptures, quilts, prints, and film – a pushback against the low expectations of the artist's 1980s Catholic childhood on a Cardiff council estate. Central was a forest of wiry twinned sculptures bearing slivers of personal photos. At 2pm each day Edwards' mother livestreamed chunks of his new radio play – based on memories such as her childhood in care, homelessness, and work as a cleaner – from her flat.
YUN HYONG-KUEN: A RETROSPECTIVE + THE FORTUNYS: A FAMILY STORY	General Exhibition **11 MAY-24 NOV 2019** 10:00-18:00 (last tickets 17:00), closed Tue **PAID ENTRY**	YUN HYONG-KUEN	First European survey of a major Korean artist, who narrowly escaped execution in 1950. His huge, brushy abstracts suggested dark portals. A separate show told the story of the Fortunys, whose innovative Venetian-made fabrics were developed in this superb palazzo.
ZIMBABWE (REPUBLIC OF) SOKO RISINA MUSORO (THE TALE WITHOUT A HEAD)	National Pavilion **11 MAY-24 NOV 2019** 10:00-18:00, closed Mon **FREE ENTRY**	GEORGINA MAXIM, NEVILLE STARLING, COSMAS SHIRIDZINOMWA, KUDZANAI VIOLET HWAMI	Titled after an epic poem by nationalist icon Herbert Chitepo, the show explored the hollowing-out of emigration, and the importance of conflict resolution. Hwami's brushy figurative paintings addressed diaspora; Maxim's intricate textiles used old clothes to evoke family; Shiridzinomwa painted harrowing political metaphors recalling Van Gogh; and Starling's dark ambrotype photos and dangling glass shards were memory made physical.

- - - - - KEY - - - - -

(123) VENICE CITY MAP (P.8–11) (A) ARSENALE MAP (P.12) (G) GIARDINI MAP (P.13)

MAP KEY	ADDRESS	NOTES	TICK IF SEEN
A	Arsenale		◯
G	Giardini		◯
G	Giardini		◯
G	Giardini		◯
71	Santa Maria Ausiliatrice, Fondamenta San Gioacchin, Castello 450		◯
72	Palazzo Fortuny, Campo San Beneto, San Marco 3958		◯
4	Istituto Santa Maria della Pietà (ground floor), Calle della Pietà, Castello 3701		◯

》ENDS

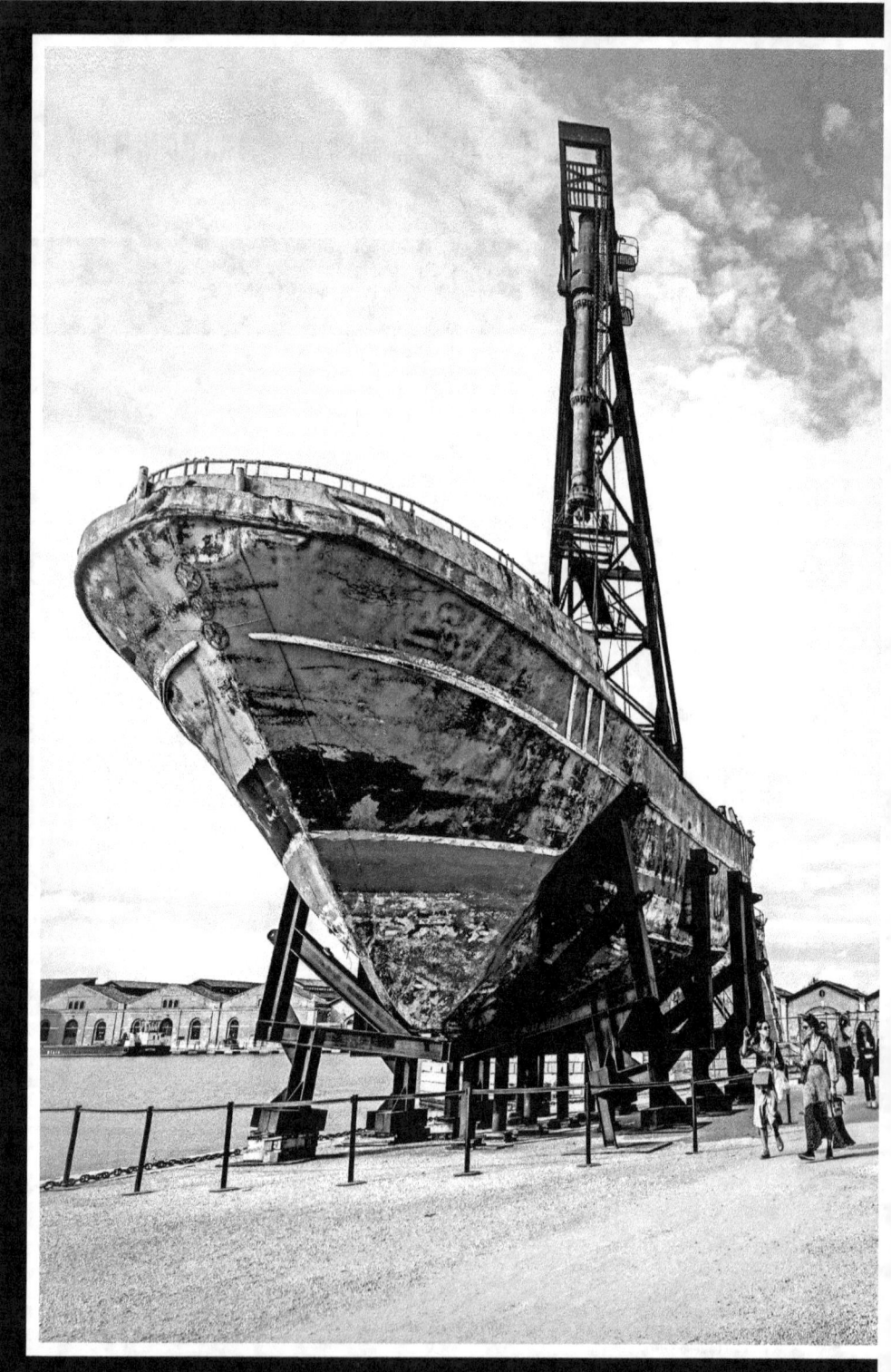

ARTIST CHECKLIST

FOR 'MAY YOU LIVE IN INTERESTING TIMES'

- -

LISTED IN ALPHABETIAL ORDER, WITH SPACE FOR COMMENTS:
ALL 84 ARTISTS FROM THE MAIN BIENNALE SHOW, SITUATED
IN THE ARSENALE AND THE GIARDINI'S CENTRAL PAVILION

- -

USING THE CHECKLIST

Every Venice Art Biennale is based around a central thematic exhibition, curated by a top art world figure. For the 2019 edition, this main show was assembled by Ralph Rugoff, then director of London's Hayward Gallery. Titled 'May You Live in Interesting Times', it was named after an apocryphal Chinese curse, and included themes of paradox, complexity, and contradiction.

There were 84 living artists exhibiting in total (or 79 if you count pairs as one artist). All had works featured in two separate sub-shows, each intended by Rugoff to have a different feel: 'Proposition A' in the Arsenale's cavernous vaults, and 'Proposition B' in the Giardini's maze-like Central Pavilion.

This section lists every exhibitor in alphabetical order of first name, with space for your own notes, plus check-boxes to tick off what has been seen in each venue – Arsenale and Giardini. At the end is a spread for further notes, with a reminder list of all the participating artists.

- - - - - FLOOR PLANS - - - - -

 ARSENALE (P.16-19)   GIARDINI (P.20-21)

Looming in front of the Arsenale's historic crane is the 2019 main show's most controversial exhibit, Christoph Büchel's 'Barca Nostra'. The boat is a recovered vessel that capsized in the Mediterranean in 2015, drowning hundreds of migrants.

ARTIST CHECKLIST

'MAY YOU LIVE IN INTERESTING TIMES' PROPOSITION A (ARSENALE) AND PROPOSITION B (GIARDINI)

≫ AD MINOLTI TO ANICKA YI

ARTIST / BIO	NOTES	TICK IF SEEN **A** IN ARSENALE **G** IN GIARDINI
AD MINOLITI (b.1980, Argentina) Lives/works: Buenos Aires		A ◯ G ◯
ALEX DA CORTE (b.1980, USA) Lives/works: Philadelphia		A ◯ G ◯
ALEX GVOJIC (b.1984, USA) Lives/works: New York *(Exhibiting with Apichatpong Weerasethakul in Arsenale)*		A ◯ G ◯
ALEXANDRA BIRCKEN (b. Germany) Lives/works: Berlin		A ◯ G ◯
ANDRA URSUȚA (b.1979, Romania) Lives/works: New York		A ◯ G ◯
ANDREAS LOLIS (b.1970, Albania) Lives/works: Athens		A ◯ G ◯
ANICKA YI (b.1971, Republic of Korea) Lives/works: New York		A ◯ G ◯

ANTHEA HAMILTON TO AVERY SINGER

ARTIST / BIO	NOTES	TICK IF SEEN ⒜ IN ARSENALE ⒢ IN GIARDINI
ANTHEA HAMILTON (b.1978, United Kingdom) Lives/works: London		A ◯ G ◯
ANTHONY HERNANDEZ (b.1947, USA) Lives/works: Los Angeles + Idaho		A ◯ G ◯
ANTOINE CATALA (b.1975, France) Lives/works: New York		A ◯ G ◯
APICHATPONG WEERASETHAKUL (b.1970, Thailand) Lives/works: Chiang Mai *(Exhibiting with Alex Gvojic in Arsenale)*		A ◯ G ◯
ARTHUR JAFA (b.1960, USA) Lives/works: Los Angeles		A ◯ G ◯
AUGUSTAS SERAPINAS (b.1990, Lithuania) Lives/works: Vilnius		A ◯ G ◯
AVERY SINGER (b.1987, USA) Lives/works: New York		A ◯ G ◯

CONTINUES OVER »

ARTIST CHECKLIST

'MAY YOU LIVE IN INTERESTING TIMES' PROPOSITION A (ARSENALE) AND PROPOSITION B (GIARDINI)

» CAMERON JAMIE TO DANH VO

ARTIST / BIO	NOTES	TICK IF SEEN A IN ARSENALE G IN GIARDINI
CAMERON JAMIE (b.1969, USA) Lives/works: Paris + Cologne		A ◯ G ◯
CAROL BOVE (b.1971, Switzerland) Lives/works: New York		A ◯ G ◯
CHRISTIAN MARCLAY (b.1955, USA) Lives/works: London		A ◯ G ◯
CHRISTINE WERTHEIM (b.1958, Australia) Lives/works: Los Angeles *(Exhibiting with Margaret Wertheim)*		A ◯ G ◯
CHRISTOPH BÜCHEL (b.1966, Switzerland) Lives/works: Reykjavik + Basel		A ◯ G ◯
CYPRIEN GAILLARD (b.1980, Berlin) Lives/works: Berlin		A ◯ G ◯
DANH VO (b.1975, Vietnam) Lives/works: Mexico City		A ◯ G ◯

》 DARREN BADER TO GEORGE CONDO

ARTIST / BIO	NOTES	TICK IF SEEN **A** IN ARSENALE **G** IN GIARDINI
DARREN BADER (b.1978, USA) Lives/works: New York + elsewhere		A ◯ G ◯
DOMINIQUE GONZALEZ-FOERSTER (b.1965, France) Lives/works: Paris *(Exhibiting with Joi Bittle in Giardini)*		A ◯ G ◯
ED ATKINS (b.1982, United Kingdom) Lives/works: Berlin + Copenhagen		A ◯ G ◯
FRIDA ORUPABO (b.1986, Norway) Lives/works: Oslo		A ◯ G ◯
GABRIEL RICO (b.1980, Mexico) Lives/works: Guadalajara		A ◯ G ◯
GAURI GILL (b.1970, India) Lives/works: New Delhi		A ◯ G ◯
GEORGE CONDO (b.1957, USA) Lives/works: New York		A ◯ G ◯

CONTINUES OVER 》

ARTIST CHECKLIST

'MAY YOU LIVE IN INTERESTING TIMES' PROPOSITION A (ARSENALE) AND PROPOSITION B (GIARDINI)

ARTIST / BIO	NOTES	TICK IF SEEN A IN ARSENALE G IN GIARDINI
HALIL ALTINDERE (b.1971, Turkey) Lives/works: Istanbul		A ☐ G ☐
HANDIWIRMAN SAPUTRA (b.1975, Indonesia) Lives/works: Yogyakarta		A ☐ G ☐
HARIS EPAMINONDA (b.1980, Republic of Cyprus) Lives/works: Berlin		A ☐ G ☐
HENRY TAYLOR (b.1958, USA) Lives/works: Los Angeles		A ☐ G ☐
HITO STEYERL (b.1966, Germany) Lives/works: Berlin		A ☐ G ☐
IAN CHENG (b.1984, USA) Lives/works: New York		A ☐ G ☐
JEAN-LUC MOULÈNE (b.1955, France) Lives/works: Paris		A ☐ G ☐

A ARSENALE FLOOR PLANS (P.16-19)   **G** GIARDINI FLOOR PLANS (P.20-21)

》 JEPPE HEIN TO JULIE MEHRETU

ARTIST / BIO	NOTES	TICK IF SEEN **A** IN ARSENALE **G** IN GIARDINI
JEPPE HEIN (b.1974, Denmark) Lives/works: Berlin		A ◯ G ◯
JESSE DARLING (b. United Kingdom) Lives/works: London + Berlin		A ◯ G ◯
JILL MULLEADY (b.1980, Uruguay) Lives/works: Los Angeles		A ◯ G ◯
JIMMIE DURHAM (b.1940, USA) Lives/works: Berlin		A ◯ G ◯
JOI BITTLE (b.1975, United States) Lives/works: New York *(Exhibiting with Dominique Gonzalez-Foerster in Giardini)*		A ◯ G ◯
JON RAFMAN (b.1981, Canada) Lives/works: Montreal		A ◯ G ◯
JULIE MEHRETU (b.1970, Ethiopia) Lives/works: New York		A ◯ G ◯

CONTINUES OVER 》

ARTIST CHECKLIST

'MAY YOU LIVE IN INTERESTING TIMES' PROPOSITION A (ARSENALE) AND PROPOSITION B (GIARDINI)

>> KAARI UPSON TO LAWRENCE ABU HAMDAN

ARTIST / BIO	NOTES	TICK IF SEEN A IN ARSENALE G IN GIARDINI
KAARI UPSON (b.1972, USA) Lives/works: Los Angeles		A ◯ G ◯
KAHLIL JOSEPH (b.1981, USA) Lives/works: Los Angeles		A ◯ G ◯
KEMANG WA LEHULERE (b.1984, Republic of South Africa) Lives/works: Cape Town		A ◯ G ◯
KHYENTSE NORBU (b.1961, Bhutan) Lives/works: India + Bhutan		A ◯ G ◯
KORAKRIT ARUNANONDCHAI (b.1986, Thailand) Lives/works: New York + Bangkok		A ◯ G ◯
LARA FAVARETTO (b.1973, Italy) Lives/works: Turin		A ◯ G ◯
LAWRENCE ABU HAMDAN (b.1985, Jordan) Lives/works: Beirut		A ◯ G ◯

- - - - - KEY - - - - -

 ARSENALE FLOOR PLANS (P.16-19) G GIARDINI FLOOR PLANS (P.20-21)

ARTIST / BIO	NOTES	TICK IF SEEN A IN ARSENALE G IN GIARDINI
LEE BUL (b.1964, Republic of Korea) Lives/works: Seoul		A ◯ G ◯
LIU WEI (b.1972, People's Republic of China) Lives/works: Beijing		A ◯ G ◯
LUDOVICA CARBOTTA (b.1982, Italy) Lives/works: Barcelona		A ◯ G ◯
MARGARET WERTHEIM (b.1958, Australia) Lives/works: Los Angeles *(Exhibiting with Christine Wertheim)*		A ◯ G ◯
MARI KATAYAMA (b.1987, Japan) Lives/works: Gunma		A ◯ G ◯
MARIA LOBODA (b.1979, Poland) Lives/works: Berlin		A ◯ G ◯
MARTINE GUTIERREZ (b.1989, USA) Lives/works: New York		A ◯ G ◯

CONTINUES OVER »

ARTIST CHECKLIST

'MAY YOU LIVE IN INTERESTING TIMES' PROPOSITION A (ARSENALE) AND PROPOSITION B (GIARDINI)

≫ MICHAEL ARMITAGE TO NJIDEKA AKUNYILI CROSBY

ARTIST / BIO	NOTES	TICK IF SEEN A IN ARSENALE G IN GIARDINI
MICHAEL ARMITAGE (b.1984, Kenya) Lives/works: London + Nairobi		A ◯ G ◯
MICHAEL E. SMITH (b.1977, USA) Lives/works: Providence, Rhode Island		A ◯ G ◯
NABUQI (b.1984, People's Republic of China) Lives/works: Beijing		A ◯ G ◯
NAIRY BAGHRAMIAN (b.1971, Iran) Lives/works: Berlin		A ◯ G ◯
NEÏL BELOUFA (b.1985, France) Lives/works: Paris		A ◯ G ◯
NICOLE EISENMAN (b.1965, France) Lives/works: New York		A ◯ G ◯
NJIDEKA AKUNYILI CROSBY (b.1983, Nigeria) Lives/works: Los Angeles		A ◯ G ◯

ARTIST / BIO	NOTES	TICK IF SEEN **A** IN ARSENALE **G** IN GIARDINI
OTOBONG NKANGA (b.1974, Nigeria) Lives/works: Antwerp		A ☐ G ☐
PENG YU (b.1974, People's Republic of China) Lives/works: Beijing *(Exhibiting with Sun Yuan)*		A ☐ G ☐
ROSEMARIE TROCKEL (b.1952, Germany) Lives/works: Cologne		A ☐ G ☐
RULA HALAWANI (b.1964, Palestine) Lives/works: Jerusalem		A ☐ G ☐
RYOJI IKEDA (b.1966, Japan) Lives/works: Paris + Kyoto		A ☐ G ☐
SHILPA GUPTA (b.1976, India) Lives/works: Mumbai		A ☐ G ☐
SLAVS AND TATARS (founded 2006) Live/Work: Berlin		A ☐ G ☐

CONTINUES OVER 》

ARTIST CHECKLIST

'MAY YOU LIVE IN INTERESTING TIMES' PROPOSITION A (ARSENALE) AND PROPOSITION B (GIARDINI)

》 SOHAM GUPTA TO TERESA MARGOLLES

ARTIST / BIO	NOTES	TICK IF SEEN **A** IN ARSENALE **G** IN GIARDINI
SOHAM GUPTA (b.1988, India) Lives/works: Kolkata		A ◯ G ◯
STAN DOUGLAS (b.1960, Canada) Lives/works: Vancouver		A ◯ G ◯
SUKI SEOKYEONG KANG (b.1977, Republic of Korea) Lives/works: Seoul		A ◯ G ◯
SUN YUAN (b.1972, People's Republic of China) Lives/works: Beijing *(Exhibiting with Peng Yu)*		A ◯ G ◯
TAREK ATOUI (b.1980, Lebanon) Lives/works: Paris		A ◯ G ◯
TAVARES STRACHAN (b.1979, The Bahamas) Lives/works: New York		A ◯ G ◯
TERESA MARGOLLES (b.1963, Mexico) Lives/works: Mexico City + Madrid		A ◯ G ◯

----- KEY -----

A ARSENALE FLOOR PLANS (P.16-19)   G GIARDINI FLOOR PLANS (P.20-21)

》 TOMÁS SARACENO TO ZHANNA KADYROVA

ARTIST / BIO	NOTES	TICK IF SEEN A IN ARSENALE G IN GIARDINI
TOMÁS SARACENO (b.1973, Argentina) Lives/works: Berlin		A ☐ G ☐
TSUYOSHI HISAKADO (b.1981, Japan) Lives/works: Kyoto		A ☐ G ☐
ULRIKE MÜLLER (b.1971, Austria) Lives/works: New York		A ☐ G ☐
YIN XIUZHEN (b.1963, People's Republic of China) Lives/works: Beijing		A ☐ G ☐
YU JI (b.1985, People's Republic of China) Lives/works: Shanghai + Vienna		A ☐ G ☐
ZANELE MUHOLI (b.1972, Republic of South Africa) Lives/works: Johannesburg + Durban + Cape Town		A ☐ G ☐
ZHANNA KADYROVA (b.1981, Ukraine) Lives/works: Kyiv		A ☐ G ☐

》 ENDS

ARTIST CHECKLIST – NOTES

'MAY YOU LIVE IN INTERESTING TIMES'
PROPOSITION A (ARSENALE)
AND PROPOSITION B (GIARDINI)

PARTICIPATING ARTISTS

AD MINOLITI	KAARI UPSON
ALEX DA CORTE	KAHLIL JOSEPH
ALEX GVOJIC	KEMANG WA LEHULERE
ALEXANDRA BIRCKEN	KHYENTSE NORBU
ANDRA URSUȚA	KORAKRIT ARUNANONDCHAI
ANDREAS LOLIS	LARA FAVARETTO
ANICKA YI	LAWRENCE ABU HAMDAN
ANTHEA HAMILTON	LEE BUL
ANTHONY HERNANDEZ	LIU WEI
ANTOINE CATALA	LUDOVICA CARBOTTA
APICHATPONG WEERASETHAKUL	MARGARET WERTHEIM
ARTHUR JAFA	MARI KATAYAMA
AUGUSTAS SERAPINAS	MARIA LOBODA
AVERY SINGER	MARTINE GUTIERREZ
CAMERON JAMIE	MICHAEL ARMITAGE
CAROL BOVE	MICHAEL E. SMITH
CHRISTIAN MARCLAY	NABUQI
CHRISTINE WERTHEIM	NAIRY BAGHRAMIAN
CHRISTOPH BÜCHEL	NEÏL BELOUFA
CYPRIEN GAILLARD	NICOLE EISENMAN
DANH VO	NJIDEKA AKUNYILI CROSBY
DARREN BADER	OTOBONG NKANGA
DOMINIQUE GONZALEZ-FOERSTER	PENG YU
ED ATKINS	ROSEMARIE TROCKEL
FRIDA ORUPABO	RULA HALAWANI
GABRIEL RICO	RYOJI IKEDA
GAURI GILL	SHILPA GUPTA
GEORGE CONDO	SLAVS AND TATARS
HALIL ALTINDERE	SOHAM GUPTA
HANDIWIRMAN SAPUTRA	STAN DOUGLAS
HARIS EPAMINONDA	SUKI SEOKYEONG KANG
HENRY TAYLOR	SUN YUAN
HITO STEYERL	TAREK ATOUI
IAN CHENG	TAVARES STRACHAN
JEAN-LUC MOULÈNE	TERESA MARGOLLES
JEPPE HEIN	TOMÁS SARACENO
JESSE DARLING	TSUYOSHI HISAKADO
JILL MULLEADY	ULRIKE MÜLLER
JIMMIE DURHAM	YIN XIUZHEN
JOI BITTLE	YU JI
JON RAFMAN	ZANELE MUHOLI
JULIE MEHRETU	ZHANNA KADYROVA

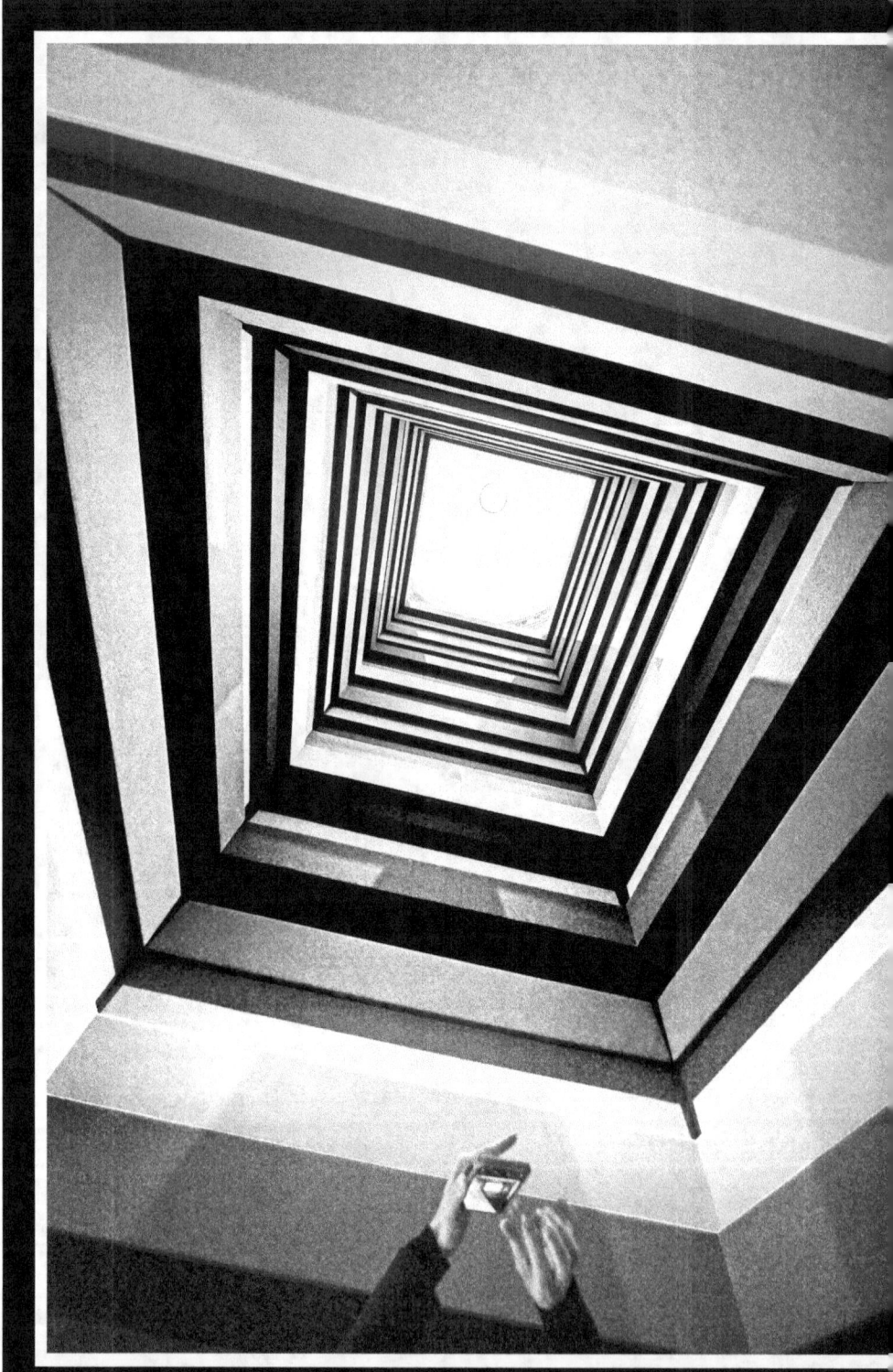

NOTEBOOK

- -
A SHORT SECTION OF LINED AND UNLINED PAGES
FOR RECORDING YOUR OWN NOTES AND VISUALS
- -

An visitor takes visual notes inside 'Opulent Ascension' (2019), a felt-clad tower rising under Abbazia San Giorgio Maggiore's dome. It was the centrepiece of Sean Scully's solo show 'Human,' one of many major independent events that coincided with the Biennale.

NOTES

NOTES

NOTES

NOTES

NOTES

NOTES

NOTES

NOTES

NOTES

NOTES

NOTES

NOTES

NOTES

NOTES

NOTES

NOTES

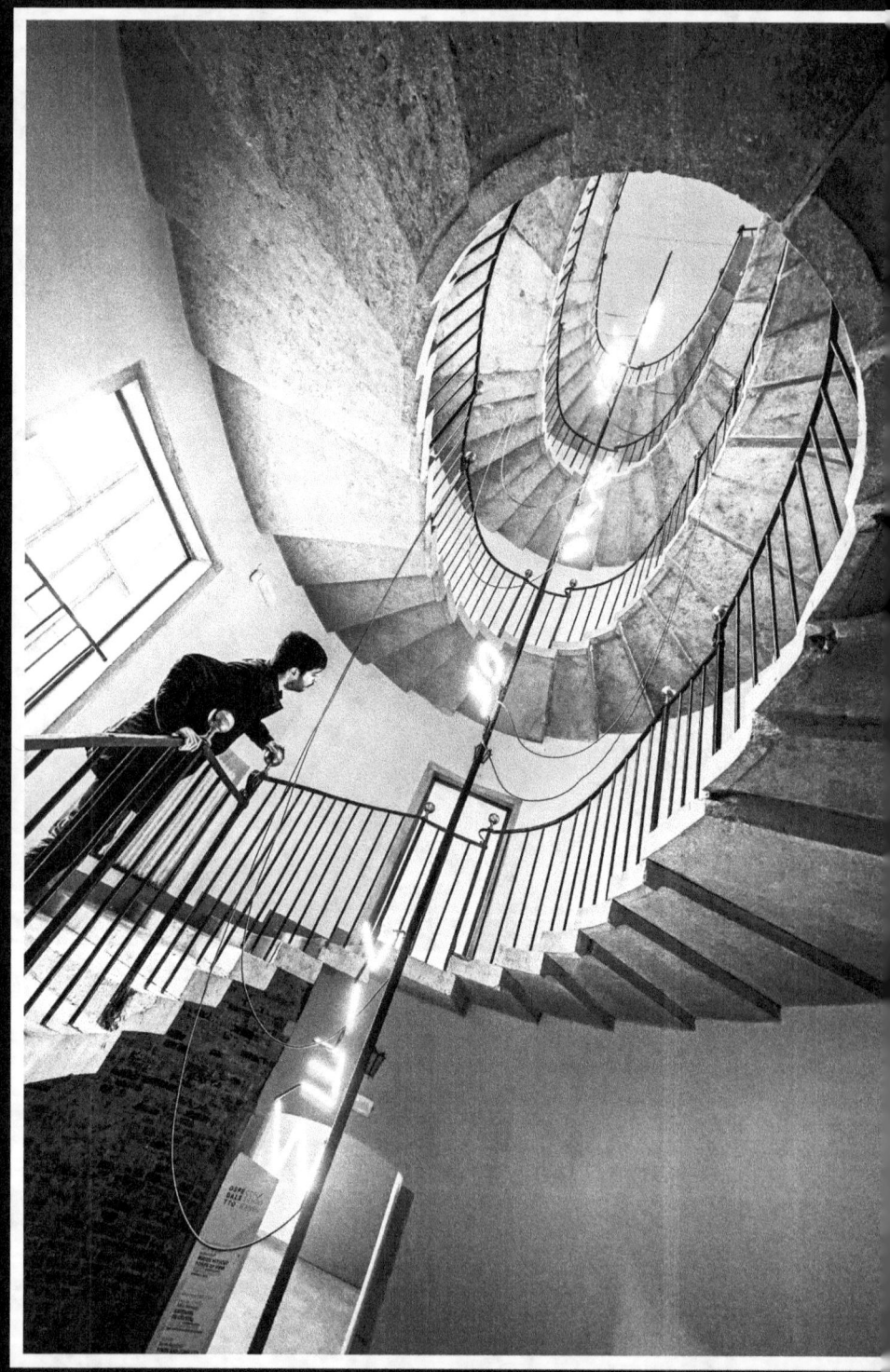

INDEX

OF ARTISTS AND VENUES

- -

QUICKLY FIND ANYTHING IN THIS BOOK, BY ARTIST NAME OR VENUE ADDRESS

- -

ARTIST INDEX: PAGE 100-117

All artists in the official Biennale events (national pavilions, collateral events, main show, performance programme, and special projects) are listed alphabetically by first name, plus headlining artists from the general exhibitions featured in this book. For quick reference, each artist's name is followed by details of the event type, pavilion nation (where applicable), exhibition title, exhibition venue, map key, and the listing's page number.

VENUE INDEX: PAGE 118-119

All the venues in this guide listed in alphabetical order, with street address, exhibition title, and map key. Also includes alternative venue titles (many Venetian place names have more than one variation), and an explanation of Venice's address system.

- - - MAPS & DIAGRAMS - - -
VENICE CITY MAP (P.8-11) ARSENALE / GIARDINI MAPS (P.12-13)
MAIN SHOW FLOOR PLANS (P.16-21)

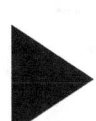

A visitor ponders Arthur Duff's 'Bodies Without Points of View' (2019), hanging in the Scala del Sardi (Sardinian Stairs) at Complesso dell'Ospedaletto. This grand venue hosted several exhibitors, including San Marino and Pablo Bronstein.

ARTIST INDEX
ALPHABETICAL BY FIRST NAME

>> STARTS

Artist / Group	Event Type	Pavilion Nation	Exhibition Title	Exhibition Venue	Map Key	Listing Page
Aanamaria Toom	National Pavilion	Kiribati	Pacific Time — Time Flies	Palazzo Mora	41	44
Aanibo Bwatanita	National Pavilion	Kiribati	Pacific Time — Time Flies	Palazzo Mora	41	44
Abdalah Abouassali	National Pavilion	Syria	Syrian Civilization is still alive	Isola di San Servolo; Chiesetta della Misericordia	13; 65	58
Ad Minoliti	Biennale Main Show		May You Live in Interesting Times	Giardini & Arsenale	G, A	66
Adrian Ghenie	General Exhibition		The Battle between Carnival and Feast	Palazzo Cini Gallery	2	24
Ahmed Abdel Karim	National Pavilion	Egypt	khnum across times witness	Giardini	G	32
Ahmed Chiha	National Pavilion	Egypt	khnum across times witness	Giardini	G	32
Alban Muja	National Pavilion	Kosovo	Family Album	Arsenale	A	44
Albert Garcia-Alzórriz	Collateral Event		Catalonia in Venice_ to lose your head (idols)	Arsenale Docks	17	30
Alberto Burri	General Exhibition		BURRI la pittura, irriducibile presenza	Fondazione Giorgio Cini Onlus	16	30
Alejandro Campins	National Pavilion	Cuba	Entorno aleccionador…	Isola di San Servolo	13	32
Aleksandar Duravcevic	Collateral Event		Artists Need to Create … Mare Nostrum	Chiesa di Santa Maria delle Penitenti	8	26
Alex Baczynski-Jenkins	Performance Programme		Meetings on Art	Teatro Piccolo	49	48
Alex Da Corte	Biennale Main Show		May You Live in Interesting Times	Giardini & Arsenale	G, A	66
Alex Gvojic	Biennale Main Show		May You Live in Interesting Times	Giardini & Arsenale	G, A	66
Alex Hérnandez	National Pavilion	Cuba	Entorno aleccionador…	Isola di San Servolo	13	32
Alex Katz	Collateral Event		Artists Need to Create … Mare Nostrum	Chiesa di Santa Maria delle Penitenti	8	26
Alexander Shishkin-Hokusai	National Pavilion	Russia	Lc 15:11—32	Giardini	G	54
Alexander Sokurov	National Pavilion	Russia	Lc 15:11—32	Giardini	G	54
Alexandra Bircken	Biennale Main Show		May You Live in Interesting Times	Giardini & Arsenale	G, A	66
Alfred Jensen	Collateral Event		Artists Need to Create … Mare Nostrum	Chiesa di Santa Maria delle Penitenti	8	26
Alfred Ullrich	Collateral Event		FutuRoma	Fondamenta Zattere (No. 417)	28	36
Ali Meer Azimi	National Pavilion	Iran	of being and singing	Fondaco Marcello	36	40
Alia Farid	Collateral Event		Future Generation Art Prize 2019 @ Venice	IUAV University of Venice	27	36
All artists of Ukraine	National Pavilion	Ukraine	The Shadow of Dream…	Arsenale	A	60
Alva Noto (Carsten Nicolai)	National Pavilion	Mongolia	A Temporality	Bruchium Fermentum	50	48
Amy Cannestra	National Pavilion	Grenada	Epic Memory	Palazzo Albrizzi-Capello	20	38
Amy Sillman	Collateral Event		Artists Need to Create … Mare Nostrum	Chiesa di Santa Maria delle Penitenti	8	26
Ananias Leki Dago	National Pavilion	Ivory Coast	The Open Shadows of Memory	Castello Gallery	37	42
Andra Ursuţa	Biennale Main Show		May You Live in Interesting Times	Giardini & Arsenale	G, A	66
Andrea Robbins	Collateral Event		Artists Need to Create … Mare Nostrum	Chiesa di Santa Maria delle Penitenti	8	26
Andreas Lolis	Biennale Main Show		May You Live in Interesting Times	Giardini & Arsenale	G, A	66
Ane Graff	National Pavilion	Nordic Countries	Weather Report: Forecasting Future	Giardini	G	50

》 CONTINUED

Artist / Group	Event Type	Pavilion Nation	Exhibition Title	Exhibition Venue	Map Key	Listing Page
Angela Vettese	Performance Programme		Meetings on Art	Teatro Piccolo	49	48
Angelica Mesiti	National Pavilion	Australia	Assembly	Giardini	G	26
Anicka Yi	Biennale Main Show; Performance Programme		May You Live in Interesting Times; Meetings on Art	Giardini & Arsenale; Teatro Piccolo	G, A 49	66; 48
Anja Radomirovic	Collateral Event		Salon Suisse: Slow	Swiss Consulate	62	54
Anna K.E.	National Pavilion	Georgia	Rearmirrorview	Arsenale	A	36
Anna Zvyagintseva	Collateral Event		Future Generation Art Prize 2019 @ Venice	IUAV University of Venice	27	36
Anonymous popular artificer	National Pavilion	Peru	Indios Antropófagos	Arsenale	A	52
Anthea Hamilton	Biennale Main Show		May You Live in Interesting Times	Giardini & Arsenale	G, A	67
Anthony Hernandez	Biennale Main Show		May You Live in Interesting Times	Giardini & Arsenale	G, A	67
Antoine Catala	Biennale Main Show		May You Live in Interesting Times	Giardini & Arsenale	G, A	67
Anurendra Jegadeva	National Pavilion	Malaysia	Holding Up a Mirror	Palazzo Malipiero	48	48
Apichatpong Weerasethakul	Biennale Main Show		May You Live in Interesting Times	Giardini & Arsenale	G, A	67
Ariamna Contino	National Pavilion	Cuba	Entorno aleccionador....	Isola di San Servolo	13	32
Arin Tikiraua	National Pavilion	Kiribati	Pacific Time – Time Flies	Palazzo Mora	41	44
Arshile Gorky	General Exhibition		Arshile Gorky: 1904 – 1948	Ca' Pesaro	7	26
Arthur Jafa	Biennale Main Show		May You Live in Interesting Times	Giardini & Arsenale	G, A	67
Arthur Petrosyan	National Pavilion	Armenia	Revolutionary Sensorium	Palazzo Zenobio—Collegio Armeno	6	26
Arthur Simms	Collateral Event		Artists Need to Create ... Mare Nostrum	Chiesa di Santa Maria delle Penitenti	8	26
ArtlabYerevan Artistic Group	National Pavilion	Armenia	Revolutionary Sensorium	Palazzo Zenobio—Collegio Armeno	6	26
Ashim Purkayastha	National Pavilion	India	Our time for a future caring	Arsenale	A	40
Atul Dodiya	National Pavilion	India	Our time for a future caring	Arsenale	A	40
Augustas Serapinas	Biennale Main Show		May You Live in Interesting Times	Giardini & Arsenale	G, A	67
Avery Singer	Biennale Main Show		May You Live in Interesting Times	Giardini & Arsenale	G, A	67
Aya Ben Ron	National Pavilion	Israel	Field Hospital X	Giardini	G	42
Barbara Jones-Hogu	Collateral Event		AFRICOBRA: Nation Time	Ca'Faccanon (Central Post Office)	3	24
Bárbara Wagner	National Pavilion	Brazil	Swinguerra	Giardini	G	28
Basel Abbas	Collateral Event		Future Generation Art Prize 2019 @ Venice	IUAV University of Venice	27	36
Belu-Simion Făinaru	National Pavilion	Romania	Unfinished Conversations...	Giardini; Istituto Romeno	G; 61	54
Benjamin de Burca	National Pavilion	Brazil	Swinguerra	Giardini	G	28
Benjamin Keating	Collateral Event		Artists Need to Create ... Mare Nostrum	Chiesa di Santa Maria delle Penitenti	8	26
Bertrand Gauguet	Collateral Event		Salon Suisse: Slow	Swiss Consulate	62	54
Beverly Pepper	Collateral Event		Beverly Pepper — Art in the Open	Spazia Thetis	12	28
Bill Jensen	Collateral Event		Artists Need to Create ... Mare Nostrum	Chiesa di Santa Maria delle Penitenti	8	26

ARTIST INDEX
ALPHABETICAL BY FIRST NAME

» CONTINUED

Artist / Group	Event Type	Pavilion Nation	Exhibition Title	Exhibition Venue	Map Key	Listing Page
Billy Gerard Frank	National Pavilion	Grenada	Epic Memory	Palazzo Albrizzi–Capello	20	38
Billy Kerry	Collateral Event		FutuRoma	Fondamenta Zattere (No. 417)	28	36
Bishwajit Goswami	National Pavilion	Bangladesh	Thirst	Palazzo Zenobio—Collegio Armeno	6	26
Bo Zheng	Performance Programme		Meetings on Art	Teatro Piccolo	49	48
Bonaventure Soh Bejeng Ndikung	National Pavilion	Finland	A Greater Miracle of Perception	Giardini	G	34
boychild	Performance Programme		Meetings on Art	Teatro Piccolo	49	48
Bunny Burson	Collateral Event		Artists Need to Create . . . Mare Nostrum	Chiesa di Santa Maria delle Penitenti	8	26
Cameron Gainer	Collateral Event		Artists Need to Create . . . Mare Nostrum	Chiesa di Santa Maria delle Penitenti	8	26
Cameron Jamie	Biennale Main Show		May You Live in Interesting Times	Giardini & Arsenale	G, A	68
Camille Abele	Collateral Event		Salon Suisse: Slow	Swiss Consulate	62	54
Carol Bove	Biennale Main Show		May You Live in Interesting Times	Giardini & Arsenale	G, A	68
Carsten Nicolai (Alva Noto)	National Pavilion	Mongolia	A Temporality	Bruchium Fermentum	50	48
Catherine Contour	Collateral Event		Salon Suisse: Slow	Swiss Consulate	62	54
Cathy Wilkes	National Pavilion	Great Britain	Cathy Wilkes	Giardini	G	36
Celia Baker	Collateral Event		FutuRoma	Fondamenta Zattere (No. 417)	28	36
Céline Eidenbenz	Collateral Event		Salon Suisse: Slow	Swiss Consulate	62	54
Charlotte Laubard	Collateral Event		Salon Suisse: Slow	Swiss Consulate	62	54
Charlotte Prodger	Collateral Event		Scotland + Venice presents Charlotte Prodger: SaF05	Arsenale Docks	17	56
Cheang Shu-lea	Collateral Event		3x3x6	Palazzo delle Prigioni	1	24
Chen Chengwei	National Pavilion	San Marino	Friendship Project International	Complesso dell'Ospedaletto; Palazzo Bollani	53; 63	56
Chen Huasha	National Pavilion	Syria	Syrian Civilization is still alive	Isola di San Servolo; Chiesetta della Misericordia	13; 65	58
Chen Qi	National Pavilion	China	Re-Rui	Arsenale	A	30
Chiara Fumai	National Pavilion	Italy	Neither Nor: The Challenge to the Labyrinth	Arsenale	A	42
Chonja Lee	Collateral Event		Salon Suisse: Slow	Swiss Consulate	62	54
Chris Larson	Collateral Event		Artists Need to Create . . . Mare Nostrum	Chiesa di Santa Maria delle Penitenti	8	26
Chris Martin	Collateral Event		Artists Need to Create . . . Mare Nostrum	Chiesa di Santa Maria delle Penitenti	8	26
Christian Bendayán	National Pavilion	Peru	Indios Antropófagos	Arsenale	A	52
Christian de Boschnek	Collateral Event		Artists Need to Create . . . Mare Nostrum	Chiesa di Santa Maria delle Penitenti	8	26
Christian Marclay	Biennale Main Show		May You Live in Interesting Times	Giardini & Arsenale	G, A	68
Christine Wertheim	Biennale Main Show		May You Live in Interesting Times	Giardini & Arsenale	G, A	68
Christoforos Savva	National Pavilion	Cyprus	Untimely, Again	Associazione Culturale Spiazzi	19	32
Christoph Büchel	Biennale Main Show		May You Live in Interesting Times	Giardini & Arsenale	G, A	68

VENICE CITY MAP (P.8-11) ARSENALE /GIARDINI MAP (P.12-13) MAIN SHOW FLOOR PLANS (P.16-21)

CONTINUED

Artist / Group	Event Type	Pavilion Nation	Exhibition Title	Exhibition Venue	Map Key	Listing Page
Christopher L. Thomas	National Pavilion	Finland	A Greater Miracle of Perception	Giardini	G	34
Christopher Wessels	National Pavilion	Finland	A Greater Miracle of Perception	Giardini	G	34
Chuck Close	Collateral Event		Artists Need to Create ... Mare Nostrum	Chiesa di Santa Maria delle Penitenti	8	26
Cindy Sherman	Collateral Event		Artists Need to Create ... Mare Nostrum	Chiesa di Santa Maria delle Penitenti	8	26
Clemens Klopfenstein	Collateral Event		Salon Suisse: Slow	Swiss Consulate	62	54
Cooking Sections	Collateral Event; Performance Programme		Future Generation Art Prize 2019 @ Venice; Meetings on Art	IUAV University of Venice; Teatro Piccolo	27; 49	36; 48
Cordy Ryman	Collateral Event		Artists Need to Create ... Mare Nostrum	Chiesa di Santa Maria delle Penitenti	8	26
Cosmas Shiridzinomwa	National Pavilion	Zimbabwe	Soko Risina Musoro (The Tale without a Head)	Santa Maria della Pietà	4	62
CRS avant-garde	National Pavilion	Grenada	Epic Memory	Palazzo Albrizzi-Capello	20	38
Cy Morgan	Collateral Event		Artists Need to Create ... Mare Nostrum	Chiesa di Santa Maria delle Penitenti	8	26
Cyprien Gaillard	Biennale Main Show		May You Live in Interesting Times	Giardini & Arsenale	G, A	68
Daiga Grantiņa	National Pavilion	Latvia	Saules Suns	Arsenale	A	44
Dan Mihălţianu	National Pavilion	Romania	Unfinished Conversations...	Giardini; Istituto Romeno	G; 61	54
Dan Turner	Collateral Event		FutuRoma	Fondamenta Zattere (No. 417)	28	36
Dana Buhl	Collateral Event		Artists Need to Create ... Mare Nostrum	Chiesa di Santa Maria delle Penitenti	8	26
Dane Mitchell	National Pavilion	New Zealand	Post hoc Post Hoc (main show); plus four broadcasting masts in fake trees	Palazzina Canonica; plus four public locations in Venice	51; 51a-d	50
Danh Vo	Biennale Main Show		May You Live in Interesting Times	Giardini & Arsenale	G, A	68
Danica Dakić	National Pavilion	Bosnia & Herzegovina	Zenica Trilogy	Palazzo Francesco Molon	14	28
Daniel Dodin	National Pavilion	Seychelles	Drift	Palazzo Mora	41	56
Daniel Turner	Collateral Events		Artists Need to Create ... Mare Nostrum; Future Generation Art Prize 2019 @ Venice	Chiesa di Santa Maria delle Penitenti; IUAV University of Venice	8; 27	26; 36
Daniela Danica Tepes	National Pavilion	Kiribati	Pacific Time — Time Flies	Palazzo Mora	41	44
Daniela Ortiz	Collateral Event		Catalonia in Venice_ to lose your head (idols)	Arsenale Docks	17	30
Dario Oleaga	National Pavilion	Dominican (Republic)	Naturaleza y biodiversidad...	Palazzo Albrizzi-Capello	20	32
Dario Ortiz	National Pavilion	San Marino	Friendship Project International	Complesso dell'Ospedaletto; Palazzo Bollani	53; 63	56
Darren Bader	Biennale Main Show		May You Live in Interesting Times	Giardini & Arsenale	G, A	69
Dave Lewis	National Pavilion	Grenada	Epic Memory	Palazzo Albrizzi-Capello	20	38
David Bestué	Collateral Event		Catalonia in Venice_ to lose your head (idols)	Arsenale Docks	17	30
David Brooks	Collateral Event		Artists Need to Create ... Mare Nostrum	Chiesa di Santa Maria delle Penitenti	8	26
David Novros	Collateral Event		Artists Need to Create ... Mare Nostrum	Chiesa di Santa Maria delle Penitenti	8	26
Dean Levin	Collateral Event		Artists Need to Create ... Mare Nostrum	Chiesa di Santa Maria delle Penitenti	8	26
Delaine Le Bas	Collateral Event		FutuRoma	Fondamenta Zattere (No. 417)	28	36
Diane Pontius	Collateral Event		Artists Need to Create ... Mare Nostrum	Chiesa di Santa Maria delle Penitenti	8	26

CONTINUES OVER 》

ARTIST INDEX
ALPHABETICAL BY FIRST NAME

>> CONTINUED

Artist / Group	Event Type	Pavilion Nation	Exhibition Title	Exhibition Venue	Map Key	Listing Page
Dilara Begum Jolly	National Pavilion	Bangladesh	Thirst	Palazzo Zenobio—Collegio Armeno	6	26
Dineo Seshee Bopape	National Pavilion	South Africa	The stronger we become	Arsenale	A	58
Djordje Ozbolt	National Pavilion	Serbia	Regaining Memory Loss	Giardini	G	56
Domenico Pellegrino	National Pavilion	Bangladesh	Thirst	Palazzo Zenobio—Collegio Armeno	6	26
Dominique Gonzalez-Foerster	Biennale Main Show; Performance Programme		May You Live in Interesting Times; Meetings on Art	Giardini & Arsenale; Teatro Piccolo	G, A; 49	69; 48
Dorothea Rockburne	Collateral Event		Artists Need to Create … Mare Nostrum	Chiesa di Santa Maria delle Penitenti	8	26
Driant Zeneli	National Pavilion	Albania	Maybe the Cosmos Is Not So Extraordinary	Arsenale	A	24
Ed Atkins	Biennale Main Show		May You Live in Interesting Times	Giardini & Arsenale	G, A	69
Edmund de Waal	General Exhibition		Psalm	Museo Ebraico; Ateneo Veneto	59; 60	54
Einako Temewi	National Pavilion	Kiribati	Pacific Time – Time Flies	Palazzo Mora	41	44
EJ Hauser	Collateral Event		Artists Need to Create … Mare Nostrum	Chiesa di Santa Maria delle Penitenti	8	26
Eklekto	Collateral Event		Salon Suisse: Slow	Swiss Consulate	62	54
El Anatsui	National Pavilion	Ghana	Ghana Freedom	Arsenale	A	36
Eli Lundgaard	Collateral Event		Future Generation Art Prize 2019 @ Venice	IUAV University of Venice	27	36
Elsie Wunderlich	National Pavilion	Guatemala	Interesting State	Palazzo Albrizzi-Capello	20	38
Emilia Rigová	Collateral Event		FutuRoma	Fondamenta Zattere (No. 417)	28	36
Emilija Škarnulytè	Collateral Event		Future Generation Art Prize 2019 @ Venice	IUAV University of Venice	27	36
Emilio Vedova	General Exhibition		Emilio Vedova by Georg Baselitz	Fondazione Emilio e Annabianca Vedova	22	34
Emma Bee Bernstein	Collateral Event		Artists Need to Create … Mare Nostrum	Chiesa di Santa Maria delle Penitenti	8	26
Enrico David	National Pavilion	Italy	Neither Nor: The Challenge to the Labyrinth	Arsenale	A	42
Eric Philippoz	Collateral Event		Salon Suisse: Slow	Swiss Consulate	62	54
Ernest Dükü	National Pavilion	Ivory Coast	The Open Shadows of Memory	Castello Gallery	37	42
Eugene Lemay	Collateral Event		Artists Need to Create … Mare Nostrum	Chiesa di Santa Maria delle Penitenti	8	26
Eugenio Tibaldi	National Pavilion	Cuba	Entorno aleccionador...	Isola di San Servolo	13	32
Eva Rothschild	National Pavilion	Ireland	The Shrinking Universe	Arsenale	A	42
Eva Stefani	National Pavilion	Greece	Mr. Stigl	Giardini	G	38
Eve Stainton	Performance Programme		Meetings on Art	Teatro Piccolo	49	48
Ezequiel Taveras	National Pavilion	Dominican Republic	Naturaleza y biodiversidad...	Palazzo Albrizzi-Capello	20	32
Farideh Lashai	Collateral Event		The Spark Is You: Parasol Unit in Venice	Benedetto Marcello Conservatory	68	60
Fei Jun	National Pavilion	China	Re-Ruì	Arsenale	A	30
Felicia Abban	National Pavilion	Ghana	Ghana Freedom	Arsenale	A	36
Filipe Branquinho	National Pavilion	Mozambique	The Past, the Present and The in Between	Palazzo Mora	41	50

》 CONTINUED

Artist / Group	Event Type	Pavilion Nation	Exhibition Title	Exhibition Venue	Map Key	Listing Page
Flavio Favelli	General Exhibition		Flavio Favelli: Il bello inverso	Ca' Rezzonico	24	34
Florence Peake	Performance Programme		Meetings on Art	Teatro Piccolo	49	48
Francesc Torres	Collateral Event		Catalonia in Venice_ to lose your head (idols)	Arsenale Docks	17	30
Franco Marrocco	National Pavilion	Bangladesh	Thirst	Palazzo Zenobio—Collegio Armeno	6	26
Franco Rota Candiani	National Pavilion	Grenada	Epic Memory	Palazzo Albrizzi-Capello	20	38
Frank Auerbach	General Exhibition		Frank Auerbach: From Painting to Drawing	Alma Zevi	26	34
Frank Walter	National Pavilion	Antigua & Barbuda	Find Yourself: Carnival and Resistance	Centro Culturale Don Orione	5	24
Frida Orupabo	Biennale Main Show		May You Live in Interesting Times	Giardini & Arsenale	G, A	69
Fuminori Nousaku	National Pavilion	Japan	Cosmo-Eggs	Giardini	G	42
Gabriel López	National Pavilion	Venezuela	Metaphor of three windows	Giardini	G	62
Gabriel Rico	Biennale Main Show		May You Live in Interesting Times	Giardini & Arsenale	G, A	69
Gabriele Gambuti	National Pavilion	San Marino	Friendship Project International	Complesso dell'Ospedaletto; Palazzo Bollani	53; 63	56
Gabrielle Goliath	Collateral Event		Future Generation Art Prize 2019 @ Venice	IUAV University of Venice	27	36
Gagik Charchyan	National Pavilion	Armenia	Revolutionary Sensorium	Palazzo Zenobio—Collegio Armeno	6	26
Gala Porras-Kim	Collateral Event		Future Generation Art Prize 2019 @ Venice	IUAV University of Venice	27	36
Gauri Gill	Biennale Main Show		May You Live in Interesting Times	Giardini & Arsenale	G, A	69
Geng Xue	National Pavilion	China	Re-Rui	Arsenale	A	30
Georg Baselitz	Collateral Event		Baselitz — Academy	Gallerie dell' Accademia	10	28
George Camille	National Pavilion	Seychelles	Drift	Palazzo Mora	41	56
George Condo	Biennale Main Show		May You Live in Interesting Times	Giardini & Arsenale	G, A	69
Georgina Maxim	National Pavilion	Zimbabwe	Soko Risina Musoro (The Tale without a Head)	Santa Maria della Pietà	4	62
Gerald Williams	Collateral Event		AFRICOBRA: Nation Time	Ca'Faccanon (Central Post Office)	3	24
Giacomo Braglia	National Pavilion	Syria	Syrian Civilization is still alive	Isola di San Servolo; Chiesetta della Misericordia	13; 65	58
Giovanna Esposito Yussif	National Pavilion	Finland	A Greater Miracle of Perception	Giardini	G	34
Giovanna Fra	National Pavilion	San Marino	Friendship Project International	Complesso dell'Ospedaletto; Palazzo Bollani	53; 63	56
Gisella Battistini	National Pavilion	San Marino	Friendship Project International	Complesso dell'Ospedaletto; Palazzo Bollani	53; 63	56
Giuseppe Biasio	National Pavilion	Syria	Syrian Civilization is still alive	Isola di San Servolo; Chiesetta della Misericordia	13; 65	58
Gonçalo Mabunda	National Pavilion	Mozambique	The Past, the Present and The in Between	Palazzo Mora	41	50
GR Iranna	National Pavilion	India	Our time for a future caring	Arsenale	A	40
Guido Bondolf	Collateral Event		Salon Suisse: Slow	Swiss Consulate	62	54
Günther Förg	Collateral Event		Förg in Venice	Palazzo Contarini Polignac	25	34

ARTIST INDEX
ALPHABETICAL BY FIRST NAME

» CONTINUED

Artist / Group	Event Type	Pavilion Nation	Exhibition Title	Exhibition Venue	Map Key	Listing Page
H.H.Lim	National Pavilion	Malaysia	Holding Up a Mirror	Palazzo Malipiero	48	48
Halil Altındere	Biennale Main Show		May You Live in Interesting Times	Giardini & Arsenale	G, A	70
Hamish Fulton	Collateral Event		Salon Suisse: Slow	Swiss Consulate	62	54
Handiwirman Saputra	Biennale Main Show; National Pavilion	Indonesia	May You Live in Interesting Times; Lost Verses	Giardini & Arsenale; Arsenale	G, A; A	70; 40
Hans Meebush	Collateral Event		Artists Need to Create … Mare Nostrum	Chiesa di Santa Maria delle Penitenti	8	26
Hans Namuth	Collateral Event		Artists Need to Create … Mare Nostrum	Chiesa di Santa Maria delle Penitenti	8	26
Hans Ulrich Obrist	Collateral Event		Salon Suisse: Slow	Swiss Consulate	62	54
Harald Thys	National Pavilion	Belgium	Mondo Cane	Giardini	G	28
Haris Epaminonda	Biennale Main Show		May You Live in Interesting Times	Giardini & Arsenale	G, A	70
Hassan Blasim	National Pavilion	Finland	A Greater Miracle of Perception	Giardini	G	34
He Xiangyu	National Pavilion	China	Re-Rui	Arsenale	A	30
Heidi Fosli	National Pavilion	Bangladesh	Thirst	Palazzo Zenobio—Collegio Armeno	6	26
Heidi Lau	Collateral Event		Heidi Lau: Apparition	Campo della Tana	32	38
Helen Frankenthaler	General Exhibition		Pittura/Panorama: Paintings	Palazzo Grimani	58	52
Helen Hirsch	Collateral Event		Salon Suisse: Slow	Swiss Consulate	62	54
Helen Mayer Harrison	Collateral Event		Artists Need to Create … Mare Nostrum	Chiesa di Santa Maria delle Penitenti	8	26
Henry Taylor	Biennale Main Show		May You Live in Interesting Times	Giardini & Arsenale	G, A	70
Heritage Artisans	National Pavilion	Antigua & Barbuda	Find Yourself: Carnival and Resistance	Centro Culturale Don Orione Artigianelli	5	24
Hito Steyerl	Biennale Main Show		May You Live in Interesting Times	Giardini & Arsenale	G, A	70
Hovhannes Margaryan	National Pavilion	Armenia	Revolutionary Sensorium	Palazzo Zenobio—Collegio Armeno	6	26
Hrafnhildur Arnardóttir (Shoplifter)	National Pavilion	Iceland	Chromo Sapiens	Spazio Punch	34	40
Hulda Guzmán	National Pavilion	Dominican Republic	Naturaleza y biodiversidad…	Palazzo Albrizzi-Capello	20	32
Hwayeon Nam	National Pavilion	Korea	History Has Failed Us, but No Matter	Giardini	G	44
Ian Cheng	Biennale Main Show		May You Live in Interesting Times	Giardini & Arsenale	G, A	70
Ibrahim Al Hamid	National Pavilion	Syria	Syrian Civilization is still alive	Isola di San Servolo; Chiesetta della Misericordia	13; 65	58
Ibrahim Mahama	National Pavilion	Ghana	Ghana Freedom	Arsenale	A	36
Igor Grubić	National Pavilion	Croatia	Traces of Disappearing (In Three Acts)	Calle della Regina (No. 2258)	18	30
İnci Eviner	National Pavilion	Turkey	We, Elsewhere	Arsenale	A	60
Ingela Ihrman	National Pavilion	Nordic Countries	Weather Report: Forecasting Future	Giardini	G	50
Intangible Cultural	National Pavilion	Antigua & Barbuda	Find Yourself: Carnival and Resistance	Centro Culturale Don Orione	5	24
Invernomuto	Performance Programme		Meetings on Art	Teatro Piccolo	49	48
Ioanna Francis	National Pavilion	Kiribati	Pacific Time – Time Flies	Palazzo Mora	41	44

» CONTINUED

Artist / Group	Event Type	Pavilion Nation	Exhibition Title	Exhibition Venue	Map Key	Listing Page
Iran do Espírito Santo	Collateral Event		Artists Need to Create … Mare Nostrum	Chiesa di Santa Maria delle Penitenti	8	26
Iris Kensmil	National Pavilion	Netherlands	The Measurement of Presence	Giardini	G	50
Isabel Lewis	Collateral Event		Salon Suisse: Slow	Swiss Consulate	62	54
Isabelle Alfonsi	Collateral Event		Salon Suisse: Slow	Swiss Consulate	62	54
Islam Abdullah	National Pavilion	Egypt	khnum across times witness	Giardini	G	32
Isuma	National Pavilion	Canada	Isuma	Giardini	G	30
Itziar Okariz	National Pavilion	Spain	Perforated	Giardini	G	58
Ivan Lam	National Pavilion	Malaysia	Holding Up a Mirror	Palazzo Malipiero	48	48
Jack Whitten	Collateral Event		Artists Need to Create … Mare Nostrum	Chiesa di Santa Maria delle Penitenti	8	26
Jae Jarrell	Collateral Event		AFRICOBRA: Nation Time	Ca'Faccanon (Central Post Office)	3	24
Jakob Steensen	Collateral Event		Future Generation Art Prize 2019 @ Venice	IUAV University of Venice	27	36
James Darling	Collateral Event		Living Rocks: A Fragment of the Universe	Magazzino del Sale No. 5	44	46
James Lee Byars	Collateral Event		The Death of James Lee Byars	Chiesa di Santa Maria della Visitazione	67	60
James Powers	Collateral Event		Artists Need to Create … Mare Nostrum	Chiesa di Santa Maria delle Penitenti	8	26
James Prosek	Collateral Event		Artists Need to Create … Mare Nostrum	Chiesa di Santa Maria delle Penitenti	8	26
Ján Berky	Collateral Event		FutuRoma	Fondamenta Zattere (No. 417)	28	36
Jane Jin Kaisen	National Pavilion	Korea	History Has Failed Us, but No Matter	Giardini	G	44
Jannis Kounellis	General Exhibition		Jannis Kounellis	Fondazione Prada	38	42
Jantsankhorol Erdenebayar	National Pavilion	Mongolia	A Temporality	Bruchium Fermentum	50	48
Jean (Hans) Arp	General Exhibition		The Nature of Arp	Peggy Guggenheim Collection	55	60
Jean Dubuffet	General Exhibition		Jean Dubuffet and Venice	ACP Palazzo Franchetti	39	42
Jean Ulrick Désert	National Pavilion	Haiti (cancelled)	The Spectacle of Tragedy	Circolo Ufficiali Marina	30	38
Jean-Luc Moulène	Biennale Main Show		May You Live in Interesting Times	Giardini & Arsenale	G, A	70
Jeff Donaldson	Collateral Event		AFRICOBRA: Nation Time	Ca'Faccanon (Central Post Office)	3	24
Jens W. Beyrich	National Pavilion	San Marino	Friendship Project International	Complesso dell'Ospedaletto; Palazzo Bollani	53; 63	56
Jeppe Hein	Biennale Main Show		May You Live in Interesting Times	Giardini & Arsenale	G, A	71
Jérémie Gindre	Collateral Event		Salon Suisse: Slow	Swiss Consulate	62	54
Jesse Darling	Biennale Main Show		May You Live in Interesting Times	Giardini & Arsenale	G, A	71
Jill Mulleady	Biennale Main Show		May You Live in Interesting Times	Giardini & Arsenale	G, A	71
Jimmie Durham	Biennale Main Show		May You Live in Interesting Times	Giardini & Arsenale	G, A	71
Jitish Kallat	National Pavilion	India	Our time for a future caring	Arsenale	A	40
Joan Jonas	General Exhibition		Joan Jonas: Moving Off the Land II	Chiesa di San Lorenzo	40	44
Joanna Pousette-Dart	Collateral Event		Artists Need to Create … Mare Nostrum	Chiesa di Santa Maria delle Penitenti	8	26

CONTINUES OVER »

ARTIST INDEX
ALPHABETICAL BY FIRST NAME

» CONTINUED

Artist / Group	Event Type	Pavilion Nation	Exhibition Title	Exhibition Venue	Map Key	Listing Page
Joe Bradley	Collateral Event		Artists Need to Create … Mare Nostrum	Chiesa di Santa Maria delle Penitenti	8	26
Joël Andrianomearisoa	National Pavilion	Madagascar	I have forgotten the night	Arsenale	A	46
John Akomfrah	National Pavilion	Ghana	Ghana Freedom	Arsenale	A	36
Joi Bittle	Biennale Main Show		May You Live in Interesting Times	Giardini & Arsenale	G, A	71
Jon Rafman	Biennale Main Show		May You Live in Interesting Times	Giardini & Arsenale	G, A	71
Jonas Mekas	Collateral Event		Artists Need to Create … Mare Nostrum	Chiesa di Santa Maria delle Penitenti	8	26
Jörg Immendorff	Collateral Event		Ichich - Ichihr - Ichwir / We All Have to Die	Fondazione Querini Stampalia	35	40
Jos de Gruyter	National Pavilion	Belgium	Mondo Cane	Giardini	G	28
Joseph Seton	National Pavilion	Antigua & Barbuda	Find Yourself: Carnival and Resistance	Centro Culturale Don Orione	5	24
Joyce Robins	Collateral Event		Artists Need to Create … Mare Nostrum	Chiesa di Santa Maria delle Penitenti	8	26
Julian Charrière	Collateral Event		Artists Need to Create … Mare Nostrum	Chiesa di Santa Maria delle Penitenti	8	26
Julie Mehretu	Biennale Main Show		May You Live in Interesting Times	Giardini & Arsenale	G, A	71
Julio Valdez	National Pavilion	Dominican Republic	Naturaleza y biodiversidad…	Palazzo Albrizzi-Capello	20	32
Justin Brice Guariglia	Collateral Event		Artists Need to Create … Mare Nostrum	Chiesa di Santa Maria delle Penitenti	8	26
Kaari Upson	Biennale Main Show		May You Live in Interesting Times	Giardini & Arsenale	G, A	72
Kaeka Michael Betero	National Pavilion	Kiribati	Pacific Time – Time Flies	Palazzo Mora	41	44
Kaeriti Baanga	National Pavilion	Kiribati	Pacific Time – Time Flies	Palazzo Mora	41	44
Kaeua Kobaua	National Pavilion	Kiribati	Pacific Time – Time Flies	Palazzo Mora	41	44
Kahlil Joseph	Biennale Main Show		May You Live in Interesting Times	Giardini & Arsenale	G, A	72
Kairaken Betio Group	National Pavilion	Kiribati	Pacific Time – Time Flies	Palazzo Mora	41	44
Kanan Aliyev	National Pavilion	Azerbaijan	Virtual Reality	Palazzo Lezze	9	26
Kasper Bosmans	Collateral Event		Future Generation Art Prize 2019 @ Venice	IUAV University of Venice	27	36
Katanuti Francis	National Pavilion	Kiribati	Pacific Time – Time Flies	Palazzo Mora	41	44
Katherine Bradford	Collateral Event		Artists Need to Create … Mare Nostrum	Chiesa di Santa Maria delle Penitenti	8	26
Kaumai Kaoma	National Pavilion	Kiribati	Pacific Time – Time Flies	Palazzo Mora	41	44
Kazumi Tanaka	Collateral Event		Artists Need to Create … Mare Nostrum	Chiesa di Santa Maria delle Penitenti	8	26
Kemang Wa Lehulere	Biennale Main Show		May You Live in Interesting Times	Giardini & Arsenale	G, A	72
Kenneth Goldsmith	General Exhibition		Hillary: The Hillary Clinton Emails	Despar Teatro Italia	33	38
Kenneth Ioane	National Pavilion	Kiribati	Pacific Time – Time Flies	Palazzo Mora	41	44
Khadar Ahmed	National Pavilion	Finland	A Greater Miracle of Perception	Giardini	G	34
Khyentse Norbu	Biennale Main Show		May You Live in Interesting Times	Giardini & Arsenale	G, A	72
Kiki Smith	Collateral Event		Artists Need to Create … Mare Nostrum	Chiesa di Santa Maria delle Penitenti	8	26
Kimsooja	Collateral Event		Salon Suisse: Slow	Swiss Consulate	62	54

▶ CONTINUED

Artist / Group	Event Type	Pavilion Nation	Exhibition Title	Exhibition Venue	Map Key	Listing Page
Klára Lakatos	Collateral Event		FutuRoma	Fondamenta Zattere (No. 417)	28	36
Klitsa Antoniou	National Pavilion	Malta	Maleth / Haven / Port	Arsenale	A	48
Konstantin Selikhanov	National Pavilion	Belarus	Exit / Uscita	Spazio Liquido	11	28
Korakrit Arunanondchai	Collateral Event		Future Generation Art Prize 2019 @ Venice	IUAV University of Venice	27	36
Korakrit Arunanondchai	Biennale Main Show		May You Live in Interesting Times	Giardini & Arsenale	G, A	72
Koushna Navabi	Collateral Event		The Spark Is You: Parasol Unit in Venice	Benedetto Marcello Conservatory	68	60
Kris Lemsalu	National Pavilion	Estonia	Birth V	Legno & Legno	23	34
Krit Ngamsom	National Pavilion	Thailand	The Revolving World	In Paradiso Art Gallery	66	58
Kudzanai Violet Hwami	National Pavilion	Zimbabwe	Soko Risina Musoro (The Tale without a Head)	Santa Maria della Pietà	4	62
Lara Favaretto	Biennale Main Show; Performance Programme		May You Live in Interesting Times; Meetings on Art	Giardini & Arsenale; Teatro Piccolo	G, A; 49	72; 48
Larissa Sansour	National Pavilion	Denmark	Heirloom	Giardini	G	32
László Varga	Collateral Event		FutuRoma	Fondamenta Zattere (No. 417)	28	36
Laura Huertas Millán	Collateral Event		Future Generation Art Prize 2019 @ Venice	IUAV University of Venice	27	36
Laure Prouvost	National Pavilion	France	Deep see blue surrounding you	Giardini	G	34
Lauren Bon	Collateral Event		Artists Need to Create . . . Mare Nostrum	Chiesa di Santa Maria delle Penitenti	8	26
Laurence Wagner	Collateral Event		Salon Suisse: Slow	Swiss Consulate	62	54
Lawrence Abu Hamdan	Biennale Main Show		May You Live in Interesting Times	Giardini & Arsenale	G, A	72
Lazar Lyutakov	National Pavilion	Bulgaria	How We Live	Fondazione Ugo e Olga Levi Onlus	15	30
Lee Bul	Biennale Main Show		May You Live in Interesting Times	Giardini & Arsenale	G, A	73
Leena Pukki	National Pavilion	Finland	A Greater Miracle of Perception	Giardini	G	34
Leonor Antunes	National Pavilion	Portugal	a seam, a surface, a hinge or a knot	Fondazione Ugo e Olga Levi Onlus	15	54
Lesley Forwood	Collateral Event		Living Rocks: A Fragment of the Universe	Magazzino del Sale No. 5	44	46
Letizia Battaglia	General Exhibition		Letizia Battaglia: Photography as a Life Choice	Casa dei Tre Oci	42	44
Li Geng	National Pavilion	San Marino	Friendship Project International	Complesso dell'Ospedaletto; Palazzo Bollani	53; 63	56
Liliana Moro	National Pavilion	Italy	Neither Nor: The Challenge to the Labyrinth	Arsenale	A	42
Lina Lapelyte	National Pavilion	Lithuania	Sun & Sea (Marina)	Marina Militare	43	44
Lisa Yuskavage	Collateral Event		Artists Need to Create . . . Mare Nostrum	Chiesa di Santa Maria delle Penitenti	8	26
Liu Wei	Biennale Main Show		May You Live in Interesting Times	Giardini & Arsenale	G, A	73
Lola Lasurt	Collateral Event		Catalonia in Venice_ to lose your head (idols)	Arsenale Docks	17	30
Lore Bert	General Exhibition		Lore Bert: Illumination. Ways to Eureka	Chiesa di San Samuele	45	46
Loren Munk	Collateral Event		Artists Need to Create . . . Mare Nostrum	Chiesa di Santa Maria delle Penitenti	8	26
Lorenzo Sandoval	National Pavilion	Finland	A Greater Miracle of Perception	Giardini	G	34

CONTINUES OVER »

ARTIST INDEX

ALPHABETICAL BY FIRST NAME

>> CONTINUED

Artist / Group	Event Type	Pavilion Nation	Exhibition Title	Exhibition Venue	Map Key	Listing Page
Louis Block	Collateral Event		Artists Need to Create … Mare Nostrum	Chiesa di Santa Maria delle Penitenti	8	26
Lua Coderch	Collateral Event		Catalonia in Venice_ to lose your head (idols)	Arsenale Docks	17	30
Luc Tuymans	General Exhibition		Luc Tuymans: La Pelle	Palazzo Grassi	46	46
Ludovica Carbotta	Biennale Main Show; Special Project		May You Live in Interesting Times; Monowe (The Powder Room)	Giardini & Arsenale; Forte Marghera	G, A; -	73; 18
Luigi Pericle	General Exhibition		Luigi Pericle (1916-2001). Beyond the Visible	Fondazione Querini Stampalia	35	46
Lynette Yiadom Boakye	National Pavilion	Ghana	Ghana Freedom	Arsenale	A	36
Madison Bycroft	Collateral Event		Future Generation Art Prize 2019 @ Venice	IUAV University of Venice	27	36
Magali Le Mens	Collateral Event		Salon Suisse: Slow	Swiss Consulate	62	54
Manuel Rodríguez Lira	National Pavilion	Peru	Indios Antropófagos	Arsenale	A	52
Marcel Borràs	Collateral Event		Catalonia in Venice_ to lose your head (idols)	Arsenale Docks	17	30
Marco Godinho	National Pavilion	Luxembourg	Written by Water	Arsenale	A	46
Marco Manzo	National Pavilion	Guatemala	Interesting State	Palazzo Albrizzi-Capello	20	38
Marcus-Gunnar Pettersson	Collateral Event		FutuRoma	Fondamenta Zattere (No. 417)	28	36
Margaret Wertheim	Biennale Main Show; Performance Programme		May You Live in Interesting Times; Meetings on Art	Giardini & Arsenale; Teatro Piccolo	G, A; 49	73; 48
Margrit Lewczuk	Collateral Event		Artists Need to Create … Mare Nostrum	Chiesa di Santa Maria delle Penitenti	8	26
Marguerite Humeau	Collateral Event		Future Generation Art Prize 2019 @ Venice	IUAV University of Venice	27	36
Mari Katayama	Biennale Main Show		May You Live in Interesting Times	Giardini & Arsenale	G, A	73
Maria Loboda	Biennale Main Show		May You Live in Interesting Times	Giardini & Arsenale	G, A	73
Mariana Telleria	National Pavilion	Argentina	El nombre de un país / The Name of a Country	Arsenale	A	24
Marie Velardi	Collateral Event		Salon Suisse: Slow	Swiss Consulate	62	54
Marina Abramović	General Exhibition		Renata Morales & Marina Abramović	Ca' Rezzonico	24	54
Mark O. Justiniani	National Pavilion	Philippines	Island Weather	Arsenale	A	52
Markéta Šestáková	Collateral Event		FutuRoma	Fondamenta Zattere (No. 417)	28	36
Marko Peljhan	National Pavilion	Slovenia	Here we go again … SYSTEM 317	Arsenale	A	58
Marraffa & Casciotti	National Pavilion	Dominican Republic	Naturaleza y biodiversidad…	Palazzo Albrizzi-Capello	20	32
Martin Puryear	National Pavilion	United States of America	Liberty	Giardini	G	62
Martina Conti	National Pavilion	San Marino	Friendship Project International	Complesso dell'Ospedaletto; Palazzo Bollani	53; 63	56
Martine Gutierrez	Biennale Main Show		May You Live in Interesting Times	Giardini & Arsenale	G, A	73
Martta Tuomaala	National Pavilion	Finland	A Greater Miracle of Perception	Giardini	G	34
Maryan Abdulkarim	National Pavilion	Finland	A Greater Miracle of Perception	Giardini	G	34
Marysia Lewandowska	Performance Programme; Special Project		Meetings on Art; It's About Time	Teatro Piccolo; Arsenale	49; A	48; 18
Mas Troup	National Pavilion	Antigua & Barbuda	Find Yourself: Carnival and Resistance	Centro Culturale Don Orione	5	24

- - - - - MAPS & DIAGRAMS - - - - -

VENICE CITY MAP (P.8-11) ARSENALE /GIARDINI MAP (P.12-13) MAIN SHOW FLOOR PLANS (P.16-21)

» CONTINUED

Artist / Group	Event Type	Pavilion Nation	Exhibition Title	Exhibition Venue	Map Key	Listing Page
Matvey Levenstein	Collateral Event		Artists Need to Create … Mare Nostrum	Chiesa di Santa Maria delle Penitenti	8	26
Mauro Pinto	National Pavilion	Mozambique	The Past, the Present and The in Between	Palazzo Mora	41	50
Mawande Ka Zenzile	National Pavilion	South Africa	The stronger we become	Arsenale	A	58
Max Becher	Collateral Event		Artists Need to Create … Mare Nostrum	Chiesa di Santa Maria delle Penitenti	8	26
Maya Lin	Collateral Event		Artists Need to Create … Mare Nostrum	Chiesa di Santa Maria delle Penitenti	8	26
Merrill Wagner	Collateral Event		Artists Need to Create … Mare Nostrum	Chiesa di Santa Maria delle Penitenti	8	26
Meyer Schapiro	Collateral Event		Artists Need to Create … Mare Nostrum	Chiesa di Santa Maria delle Penitenti	8	26
Michael Armitage	Biennale Main Show		May You Live in Interesting Times	Giardini & Arsenale	G, A	74
Michael E. Smith	Biennale Main Show		May You Live in Interesting Times	Giardini & Arsenale	G, A	74
Michele Savorgnano	Collateral Event		Salon Suisse: Slow	Swiss Consulate	62	54
Miguel Ramirez	National Pavilion	Dominican Republic	Naturaleza y biodiversidad…	Palazzo Albrizzi-Capello	20	32
Mikaere Tebwebwe	National Pavilion	Kiribati	Pacific Time – Time Flies	Palazzo Mora	41	44
Miklós Onucsán	National Pavilion	Romania	Unfinished Conversations…	Giardini; Istituto Romeno	G; 61	54
Miracle Workers Collective	National Pavilion	Finland	A Greater Miracle of Perception	Giardini	G	34
Mitra Farahani	Collateral Event		The Spark Is You: Parasol Unit in Venice	Benedetto Marcello Conservatory	68	60
Monira Al Qadiri	Collateral Event		Future Generation Art Prize 2019 @ Venice	IUAV University of Venice	27	36
Morteza Ahmadvand	Collateral Event		The Spark Is You: Parasol Unit in Venice	Benedetto Marcello Conservatory	68	60
Motoyuki Shitamichi	National Pavilion	Japan	Cosmo-Eggs	Giardini	G	42
nabbteeri	National Pavilion	Nordic Countries	Weather Report: Forecasting Future	Giardini	G	50
Nabuqi	Biennale Main Show		May You Live in Interesting Times	Giardini & Arsenale	G, A	74
Nada Prlja	National Pavilion	North Macedonia	Subversion to Red	Palazzo Rota Ivancich	52	50
Nafis Ahmed Gazi	National Pavilion	Bangladesh	Thirst	Palazzo Zenobio–Collegio Armeno	6	26
Nairy Baghramian	Biennale Main Show		May You Live in Interesting Times	Giardini & Arsenale	G, A	74
Naiza Khan	National Pavilion	Pakistan	Manora Field Notes	Tanarte / Spazio Tana	54	50
Nandalal Bose	National Pavilion	India	Our time for a future caring	Arsenale	A	40
Napoleon Jones-Henderson	Collateral Event		AFRICOBRA: Nation Time	Ca'Faccanon (Central Post Office)	3	24
Narine Arakelian	National Pavilion	Armenia	Revolutionary Sensorium	Palazzo Zenobio–Collegio Armeno	6	26
Nástio Mosquito	Performance Programme		Meetings on Art	Teatro Piccolo	49	48
Natalie Rocha Capiello	National Pavilion	Venezuela	Metaphor of three windows	Giardini	G	62
Natascha Süder Happelmann	National Pavilion	Germany	Natascha Süder Happelmann	Giardini	G	36
Nathlie Provosty	Collateral Event		Artists Need to Create … Mare Nostrum	Chiesa di Santa Maria delle Penitenti	8	26
Navid Nuur	Collateral Event		The Spark Is You: Parasol Unit in Venice	Benedetto Marcello Conservatory	68	60
Nazgol Ansarini	Collateral Event		The Spark Is You: Parasol Unit in Venice	Benedetto Marcello Conservatory	68	60

CONTINUES OVER »

ARTIST INDEX
ALPHABETICAL BY FIRST NAME

» CONTINUED

Artist / Group	Event Type	Pavilion Nation	Exhibition Title	Exhibition Venue	Map Key	Listing Page
Neil Beloufa	Biennale Main Show		May You Live in Interesting Times	Giardini & Arsenale	G, A	74
Nelson Rangelosky	National Pavilion	Venezuela	Metaphor of three windows	Giardini	G	62
Nelson Stevens	Collateral Event		AFRICOBRA: Nation Time	Ca'Faccanon (Central Post Office)	3	24
Neneia Takoikoi	National Pavilion	Kiribati	Pacific Time – Time Flies	Palazzo Mora	41	44
Nevena Puljic	Collateral Event		Salon Suisse: Slow	Swiss Consulate	62	54
Neville Starling	National Pavilion	Zimbabwe	Soko Risina Musoro (The Tale without a Head)	Santa Maria della Pietà	4	62
Newton	Collateral Event		Artists Need to Create . . . Mare Nostrum	Chiesa di Santa Maria delle Penitenti	8	26
Nicola Pica	National Pavilion	Dominican Republic	Naturaleza y biodiversidad...	Palazzo Albrizzi-Capello	20	32
Nicole Eisenman	Biennale Main Show		May You Live in Interesting Times	Giardini & Arsenale	G, A	74
Nimei Itinikarawa	National Pavilion	Kiribati	Pacific Time – Time Flies	Palazzo Mora	41	44
Njideka Akunyili Crosby	Biennale Main Show		May You Live in Interesting Times	Giardini & Arsenale	G, A	74
Nkisi	Performance Programme		Meetings on Art	Teatro Piccolo	49	48
Norman Cohn	National Pavilion	Canada	Isuma	Giardini	G	30
Nujoom Alghanem	National Pavilion	United Arab Emirates	Passage	Arsenale	A	62
Obeta Taia	National Pavilion	Kiribati	Pacific Time – Time Flies	Palazzo Mora	41	44
Ödön Gyügyi	Collateral Event		FutuRoma	Fondamenta Zattere (No. 417)	28	36
Optics Division of The Metabolic Studio	Collateral Event		Artists Need to Create . . . Mare Nostrum	Chiesa di Santa Maria delle Penitenti	8	26
Orkhan Mammadov	National Pavilion	Azerbaijan	Virtual Reality	Palazzo Lezze	9	26
Otobong Nkanga	Biennale Main Show		May You Live in Interesting Times	Giardini & Arsenale	G, A	75
Otto Michael	National Pavilion	Peru	Indios Antropófagos	Arsenale	A	52
Outi Pieski	National Pavilion	Finland	A Greater Miracle of Perception	Giardini	G	34
Pablo Bronstein	General Exhibition		Pablo Bronstein: Carousel	Complesso dell'Ospedaletto	53	50
Pablo Vargas Lugo	National Pavilion	Mexico	Actos de Dios / Acts of God	Arsenale	A	48
Panos Charalambous	National Pavilion	Greece	Mr. Stigl	Giardini	G	38
Panya Vijinthanasarn	National Pavilion	Thailand	The Revolving World	In Paradiso Art Gallery	66	58
Paolo Baratta	Performance Programme		Meetings on Art	Teatro Piccolo	49	48
Paul Apak	National Pavilion	Canada	Isuma	Giardini	G	30
Paul Maheke	Performance Programme		Meetings on Art	Teatro Piccolo	49	48
Pauline Boudry	National Pavilion; Collateral Event	Switzerland	Moving Backwards; Salon Suisse: Slow	Giardini; Swiss Consulate	G; 62	58; 54
Pauloosie Qulitalik	National Pavilion	Canada	Isuma	Giardini	G	30
Peng Yu	Biennale Main Show		May You Live in Interesting Times	Giardini & Arsenale	G, A	75
Perejaume	Collateral Event		Catalonia in Venice_ to lose your head (idols)	Arsenale Docks	17	30

» CONTINUED

Artist / Group	Event Type	Pavilion Nation	Exhibition Title	Exhibition Venue	Map Key	Listing Page
Peter Acheson	Collateral Event		Artists Need to Create … Mare Nostrum	Chiesa di Santa Maria delle Penitenti	8	26
Peter Lamborn Wilson	Collateral Event		Artists Need to Create … Mare Nostrum	Chiesa di Santa Maria delle Penitenti	8	26
Philippe Parreno	Collateral Event		Philippe Parreno	Espace Louis Vuitton Venice	56	52
Philippe Shangti	National Pavilion	Andorra	The Future Is Now	Santa Maria della Pietà	4	24
Phong Bui	Collateral Event		Artists Need to Create … Mare Nostrum	Chiesa di Santa Maria delle Penitenti	8	26
Pino Pascali	Collateral Event		Pino Pascali. From image to form	Palazzo Cavanis	57	52
Preema Nazia Andaleeb	National Pavilion	Bangladesh	Thirst	Palazzo Zenobio—Collegio Armeno	6	26
Primo Vanadia	National Pavilion	Syria	Syrian Civilization is still alive	Isola di San Servolo; Chiesetta della Misericordia	13; 65	58
Ra Kajol	National Pavilion	Bangladesh	Thirst	Palazzo Zenobio—Collegio Armeno	6	26
Raatu Tiuteke	National Pavilion	Kiribati	Pacific Time – Time Flies	Palazzo Mora	41	44
Rada Boukova	National Pavilion	Bulgaria	How We Live	Fondazione Ugo e Olga Levi Onlus	15	30
Rairauea Rue	National Pavilion	Kiribati	Pacific Time – Time Flies	Palazzo Mora	41	44
Ralph Rugoff	Performance Programme		Meetings on Art	Teatro Piccolo	49	48
Ramin & Reda	Collateral Event		Salon Suisse: Slow	Swiss Consulate	62	54
Remy Jungerman	National Pavilion	Netherlands	The Measurement of Presence	Giardini	G	50
Renata Morales	General Exhibition		Renata Morales & Marina Abramović	Ca' Rezzonico	24	54
Renate Bertlmann	National Pavilion	Austria	Discordo Ergo Sum	Giardini	G	26
Renate Lorenz	National Pavilion; Collateral Event	Switzerland	Moving Backwards; Salon Suisse: Slow	Giardini; Swiss Consulate	G; 62	58; 54
Renate Ponsold	Collateral Event		Artists Need to Create … Mare Nostrum	Chiesa di Santa Maria delle Penitenti	8	26
Reza Lavassani	National Pavilion	Iran	of being and singing	Fondaco Marcello	36	40
Ricardo García	National Pavilion	Venezuela	Metaphor of three windows	Giardini	G	62
Riccardo Caldura	Collateral Event		Salon Suisse: Slow	Swiss Consulate	62	54
Richard Nielsen	Collateral Event		Artists Need to Create … Mare Nostrum	Chiesa di Santa Maria delle Penitenti	8	26
Rirkrit Tiravanija	Collateral Event		Artists Need to Create … Mare Nostrum	Chiesa di Santa Maria delle Penitenti	8	26
Rita Bertrecchi	National Pavilion	Dominican Republic	Naturaleza y biodiversidad…	Palazzo Albrizzi-Capello	20	32
Roberto Miniati	National Pavilion	Grenada	Epic Memory	Palazzo Albrizzi-Capello	20	38
Robin Michel	Collateral Event		Salon Suisse: Slow	Swiss Consulate	62	54
Rodrigo Hernández	Collateral Event		Future Generation Art Prize 2019 @ Venice	IUAV University of Venice	27	36
Roman Stańczak	National Pavilion	Poland	Flight	Giardini	G	52
Ron Gorchov	Collateral Event		Artists Need to Create … Mare Nostrum	Chiesa di Santa Maria delle Penitenti	8	26
Rosemarie Trockel	Biennale Main Show		May You Live in Interesting Times	Giardini & Arsenale	G, A	75
Ruanne Abou-Rahme	Collateral Event		Future Generation Art Prize 2019 @ Venice	IUAV University of Venice	27	36

CONTINUES OVER »

ARTIST INDEX
ALPHABETICAL BY FIRST NAME

>> CONTINUED

Artist / Group	Event Type	Pavilion Nation	Exhibition Title	Exhibition Venue	Map Key	Listing Page
Rugile Barzdziukaite	National Pavilion	Lithuania	Sun & Sea (Marina)	Marina Militare	43	44
Rula Halawani	Biennale Main Show		May You Live in Interesting Times	Giardini & Arsenale	G, A	75
Rummana Hussain	National Pavilion	India	Our time for a future caring	Arsenale	A	40
Runita Rabwaa	National Pavilion	Kiribati	Pacific Time – Time Flies	Palazzo Mora	41	44
Ryoji Ikeda	Biennale Main Show		May You Live in Interesting Times	Giardini & Arsenale	G, A	75
Saad Yagan	National Pavilion	Syria	Syrian Civilization is still alive	Isola di San Servolo; Chiesetta della Misericordia	13; 65	58
Saed Salloum	National Pavilion	Syria	Syrian Civilization is still alive	Isola di San Servolo; Chiesetta della Misericordia	13; 65	58
Sahand Hesamiyan	Collateral Event		The Spark Is You: Parasol Unit in Venice	Benedetto Marcello Conservatory	68	60
Samira Alikhanzadeh	National Pavilion	Iran	of being and singing	Fondaco Marcello	36	40
Sara Paolini	Collateral Event		Salon Suisse: Slow	Swiss Consulate	62	54
Sarah Sze	Collateral Event		Artists Need to Create . . . Mare Nostrum	Chiesa di Santa Maria delle Penitenti	8	26
Sean Edwards	Collateral Event		Wales in Venice: Sean Edwards	Santa Maria Ausiliatrice	71	62
Sean Scully	General Exhibition		Sean Scully: Human	Abbazia di San Giorgio Maggiore	64	56
Sebastián	National Pavilion	San Marino	Friendship Project International	Complesso dell'Ospedaletto; Palazzo Bollani	53; 63	56
Segundo Candiño Rodríguez	National Pavilion	Peru	Indios Antropófagos	Arsenale	A	52
Selasi Awusi Sosu	National Pavilion	Ghana	Ghana Freedom	Arsenale	A	36
Selma Selman	Collateral Event		FutuRoma	Fondamenta Zattere (No. 417)	28	36
Sergio Prego	National Pavilion	Spain	Perforated	Giardini	G	58
Serwan Baran	National Pavilion	Iraq	Fatherland	Ca' del Duca	31	40
Shahram Karimi	Collateral Event		Artists Need to Create . . . Mare Nostrum	Chiesa di Santa Maria delle Penitenti	8	26
Shakuntala Kulkarni	National Pavilion	India	Our time for a future caring	Arsenale	A	40
Shervone Neckles	National Pavilion	Grenada	Epic Memory	Palazzo Albrizzi-Capello	20	38
Shilpa Gupta	Biennale Main Show		May You Live in Interesting Times	Giardini & Arsenale	G, A	75
Shirin Neshat	Collateral Event		Artists Need to Create . . . Mare Nostrum	Chiesa di Santa Maria delle Penitenti	8	26
Shirley Tse	Collateral Event		Shirley Tse: Stakeholders, Hong Kong in Venice	Campo della Tana	32	56
Shoja Azari	Collateral Event		Artists Need to Create . . . Mare Nostrum	Chiesa di Santa Maria delle Penitenti	8	26
Shoplifter (Hrafnhildur Arnardóttir)	National Pavilion	Iceland	Chromo Sapiens	Spazio Punch	34	40
Siah Armajani	Collateral Event		The Spark Is You: Parasol Unit in Venice	Benedetto Marcello Conservatory	68	60
Sir Gerald Price	National Pavilion	Antigua & Barbuda	Find Yourself: Carnival and Resistance	Centro Culturale Don Orione	5	24
siren eun young jung	National Pavilion	Korea	History Has Failed Us, but No Matter	Giardini	G	44
Slavs and Tatars	Biennale Main Show		May You Live in Interesting Times	Giardini & Arsenale	G, A	75
Soham Gupta	Biennale Main Show		May You Live in Interesting Times	Giardini & Arsenale	G, A	76

- - - - - MAPS & DIAGRAMS - - - - -
VENICE CITY MAP (P.8-11) ARSENALE /GIARDINI MAP (P.12-13) MAIN SHOW FLOOR PLANS (P.16-21)

CONTINUED

Artist / Group	Event Type	Pavilion Nation	Exhibition Title	Exhibition Venue	Map Key	Listing Page
Somsak Chowtadapong	National Pavilion	Thailand	The Revolving World	In Paradiso Art Gallery	66	58
Sondra Perry	Collateral Event		Future Generation Art Prize 2019 @ Venice	IUAV University of Venice	27	36
Song-Ming Ang	National Pavilion	Singapore	Music For Everyone: Variations on a Theme	Arsenale	A	58
Sonya Lindfors	National Pavilion	Finland	A Greater Miracle of Perception	Giardini	G	34
Stan Douglas	Biennale Main Show		May You Live in Interesting Times	Giardini & Arsenale	G, A	76
Stanislav Kolíbal	National Pavilion	Czech & Slovak Republics	Former Uncertain Indicated	Giardini	G	32
Suki Seokyeong Kang	Biennale Main Show		May You Live in Interesting Times	Giardini & Arsenale	G, A	76
Sun Yuan	Biennale Main Show		May You Live in Interesting Times	Giardini & Arsenale	G, A	76
Suvi West	National Pavilion	Finland	A Greater Miracle of Perception	Giardini	G	34
Syagini Ratna Wulan	National Pavilion	Indonesia	Lost Verses	Arsenale	A	40
Sylvain Menetrey	Collateral Event		Salon Suisse: Slow	Swiss Consulate	62	54
Tamara Gonzales	Collateral Event		Artists Need to Create … Mare Nostrum	Chiesa di Santa Maria delle Penitenti	8	26
Tamás Waliczky	National Pavilion	Hungary	Imaginary Cameras	Giardini	G	40
Tamuera Tebebe	National Pavilion	Kiribati	Pacific Time – Time Flies	Palazzo Mora	41	44
Tang Shuangning	National Pavilion	San Marino	Friendship Project International	Complesso dell'Ospedaletto; Palazzo Bollani	53; 63	56
Tarek Atoui	Biennale Main Show		May You Live in Interesting Times	Giardini & Arsenale	G, A	76
Taro Yasuno	National Pavilion	Japan	Cosmo-Eggs	Giardini	G	42
Taus Makhacheva	Collateral Event		Future Generation Art Prize 2019 @ Venice	IUAV University of Venice	27	36
Tavares Strachan	Biennale Main Show		May You Live in Interesting Times	Giardini & Arsenale	G, A	76
Teeti Aaloa	National Pavilion	Kiribati	Pacific Time – Time Flies	Palazzo Mora	41	44
Temarewe Banaan	National Pavilion	Kiribati	Pacific Time – Time Flies	Palazzo Mora	41	44
Teniteiti Mikaere	National Pavilion	Kiribati	Pacific Time – Time Flies	Palazzo Mora	41	44
Teresa Margolles	Biennale Main Show		May You Live in Interesting Times	Giardini & Arsenale	G, A	76
Terita Itinikarawa	National Pavilion	Kiribati	Pacific Time – Time Flies	Palazzo Mora	41	44
Teroloang Borouea	National Pavilion	Kiribati	Pacific Time – Time Flies	Palazzo Mora	41	44
Teuea Kabunare	National Pavilion	Kiribati	Pacific Time – Time Flies	Palazzo Mora	41	44
Thea Tini	National Pavilion	San Marino	Friendship Project International	Complesso dell'Ospedaletto; Palazzo Bollani	53; 63	56
Timothy Payne	National Pavilion	Antigua & Barbuda	Find Yourself: Carnival and Resistance	Centro Culturale Don Orione	5	24
Tineta Timirau	National Pavilion	Kiribati	Pacific Time – Time Flies	Palazzo Mora	41	44
Tiribo Kobaua	National Pavilion	Kiribati	Pacific Time – Time Flies	Palazzo Mora	41	44
Todd Williamson	Collateral Event		Processional	Santa Maria della Pietà	4	54
Tokintekai Ekentetake	National Pavilion	Kiribati	Pacific Time – Time Flies	Palazzo Mora	41	44

CONTINUES OVER »

ARTIST INDEX

ALPHABETICAL BY FIRST NAME

>> CONTINUED

Artist / Group	Event Type	Pavilion Nation	Exhibition Title	Exhibition Venue	Map Key	Listing Page
Tom Hodgkinson	Collateral Event		Salon Suisse: Slow	Swiss Consulate	62	54
Tomás Saraceno	Biennale Main Show; Performance Programme		May You Live in Interesting Times; Meetings on Art	Giardini & Arsenale; Teatro Piccolo	G, A; 49	77; 48
Tomas Vu	Collateral Event		Artists Need to Create … Mare Nostrum	Chiesa di Santa Maria delle Penitenti	8	26
Tong Yanrunan	National Pavilion	Ivory Coast	The Open Shadows of Memory	Castello Gallery	37	42
Toshiaki Ishikura	National Pavilion	Japan	Cosmo-Eggs	Giardini	G	42
Toyin Ojih Odutola	Collateral Event		Future Generation Art Prize 2019 @ Venice	IUAV University of Venice	27	36
Tracey Rose	National Pavilion	South Africa	The stronger we become	Arsenale	A	58
Trevor Borg	National Pavilion	Malta	Maleth / Haven / Port	Arsenale	A	48
Tristan Duke	Collateral Event		Artists Need to Create … Mare Nostrum	Chiesa di Santa Maria delle Penitenti	8	26
Tristan Weddigen	Collateral Event		Salon Suisse: Slow	Swiss Consulate	62	54
Tsuyoshi Hisakado	Biennale Main Show		May You Live in Interesting Times	Giardini & Arsenale	G, A	77
Ugo Rondinone	Collateral Event		Artists Need to Create … Mare Nostrum	Chiesa di Santa Maria delle Penitenti	8	26
Ulrike Müller	Biennale Main Show		May You Live in Interesting Times	Giardini & Arsenale	G, A	77
Ulviyya Aliyeva	National Pavilion	Azerbaijan	Virtual Reality	Palazzo Lezze	9	26
Uttam Kumar Karmaker	National Pavilion	Bangladesh	Thirst	Palazzo Zenobio—Collegio Armeno	6	26
Vaiva Grainyte	National Pavilion	Lithuania	Sun & Sea (Marina)	Marina Militare	43	44
Valérie Leray	Collateral Event		FutuRoma	Fondamenta Zattere (No. 417)	28	36
Valérie Oka	National Pavilion	Ivory Coast	The Open Shadows of Memory	Castello Gallery	37	42
Vardan Jaloyan	National Pavilion	Armenia	Revolutionary Sensorium	Palazzo Zenobio—Collegio Armeno	6	26
Various artists	General Exhibition		Bivacco (Bivouac)	Isola di San Servolo	13	28
Various Artists	General Exhibition		Dysfunctional: Carpenter's Workshop	Galleria Giorgio Franchetti	21	32
Various artists	General Exhibition		Glasstress 2019 (6th edition)	Fondazione Berengo Art Space	29	36
Various artists	General Exhibition		Heartbreak	Ca' del Duca	31	38
Various artists	General Exhibition		Luogo e Segni (Place and Signs)	Punta della Dogana	47	46
Various artists	General Exhibition		Peggy Guggenheim: The Last Dogaressa	Peggy Guggenheim Collection	55	52
Various artists	General Exhibition		There Is a Beginning at the End	Chiesa di San Fantin	69	60
Various artists	General Exhibition		Time, Forward!	V-A-C Zattere	70	60
Vesko Gagović	National Pavilion	Montenegro	Odiseja / An Odyssey	Palazzo Malipiero	48	48
Victoria Mühlig	Collateral Event		Salon Suisse: Slow	Swiss Consulate	62	54

VENICE CITY MAP (P.8-11) ARSENALE /GIARDINI MAP (P.12-13) MAIN SHOW FLOOR PLANS (P.16-21)

≫ CONTINUED

Artist / Group	Event Type	Pavilion Nation	Exhibition Title	Exhibition Venue	Map Key	Listing Page
Victoria Sin	Performance Programme		Meetings on Art	Teatro Piccolo	49	48
Vidya Gastaldon	Collateral Event		Salon Suisse: Slow	Swiss Consulate	62	54
Vince Briffa	National Pavilion	Malta	Maleth / Haven / Port	Arsenale	A	48
Vincent Barras	Collateral Event		Salon Suisse: Slow	Swiss Consulate	62	54
Vivian Caccuri	Performance Programme		Meetings on Art	Teatro Piccolo	49	48
Vivien Sansour	Performance Programme		Meetings on Art	Teatro Piccolo	49	48
Voluspa Jarpa	National Pavilion	Chile	Altered Views	Arsenale	A	30
Wadsworth Jarrell	Collateral Event		AFRICOBRA: Nation Time	Ca'Faccanon (Central Post Office)	3	24
Wolfgang Laib	Collateral Event		Artists Need to Create … Mare Nostrum	Chiesa di Santa Maria delle Penitenti	8	26
Xie Tian	National Pavilion	Syria	Syrian Civilization is still alive	Isola di San Servolo; Chiesetta della Misericordia	13; 65	58
Xing Junqin	National Pavilion	San Marino	Friendship Project International	Complesso dell'Ospedaletto; Palazzo Bollani	53; 63	56
Xu de Qi	National Pavilion	San Marino	Friendship Project International	Complesso dell'Ospedaletto; Palazzo Bollani	53; 63	56
Y.Z. Kam	Collateral Event		The Spark Is You: Parasol Unit in Venice	Benedetto Marcello Conservatory	68	60
Yamandú Canosa	National Pavilion	Uruguay	La casa empática	Giardini	G	62
Yasi Alipour	Collateral Event		Artists Need to Create … Mare Nostrum	Chiesa di Santa Maria delle Penitenti	8	26
Yin Xiuzhen	Biennale Main Show		May You Live in Interesting Times	Giardini & Arsenale	G, A	77
Yu Araki	Collateral Event		Future Generation Art Prize 2019 @ Venice	IUAV University of Venice	27	36
Yu Ji	Biennale Main Show		May You Live in Interesting Times	Giardini & Arsenale	G, A	77
Yun Hyong-Kuen	General Exhibition		Yun Hyong-Kuen: A retrospective	Palazzo Fortuny	72	62
Zacharias Kunuk	National Pavilion	Canada	Isuma	Giardini	G	30
Zad Moultaka	Collateral Event		The Death of James Lee Byars	Chiesa di Santa Maria della Visitazione	67	60
Zadie Xa	Performance Programme		Meetings on Art	Teatro Piccolo	49	48
Zafos Xagoraris	National Pavilion	Greece	Mr. Stigl	Giardini	G	38
Zahrah Al Ghamdi	National Pavilion	Saudi Arabia	After Illusion	Arsenale	A	56
Zanele Muholi	Biennale Main Show		May You Live in Interesting Times	Giardini & Arsenale	G, A	77
Zarnishan Yusifova	National Pavilion	Azerbaijan	Virtual Reality	Palazzo Lezze	9	26
Zeigam Azizov	National Pavilion	Azerbaijan	Virtual Reality	Palazzo Lezze	9	26
Zhanna Kadyrova	Biennale Main Show		May You Live in Interesting Times	Giardini & Arsenale	G, A	77
Zulkifli Yusoff	National Pavilion	Malaysia	Holding Up a Mirror	Palazzo Malipiero	48	48

≫ ENDS

VENUE INDEX

VENUE – ADDRESS – EXHIBITOR – MAP KEY

CAPITALS: Primary entries with full details   **Upper and lower case:** Alternate titles, see primary entries for details

ABOUT VENICE ADDRESSES

Venice is divided into six 'sestiere', or districts: San Marco, San Polo, Santa Croce, Cannaregio, Castello, and Dorsoduro. Each has its own number sequence, with Santa Croce 55 being the building in Santa Croce numbered 55, and San Marco 55 the one in San Marco numbered 55. Islands have their own individual sequences, such as Giudecca 43 or San Pietro di Castello 40. Multiple-occupancy sites include letters, such as Dorsoduro 919/A. These numbers are displayed outside each address, usually painted on the wall, and proceed – like the streets – in a labyrinthine manner. Road names are generally added before the sestiere, to give a better idea of location; however landmarks such as churches and palazzi do not always include streets or numbers as part of their official address. Note that some street names, such as Calle del Forno, occur more than once, and online maps (not always accurate for Venice) may choose the wrong one. So it is wise to check the sestiere name as well, to ensure it is in the correct part of the island.

A long coiled cord, reminiscent of an electrical cable, hangs (aptly) in the Arsenale's Corderie. It is one of many wool sculptures from 'Crochet Coral Reef', a long-term project about global heating by Australian-born twins Christine and Margaret Wertheim.

An **ART WORLD EXPLORER** *guide*

PUBLISHED IN 2020 BY REVERSE PRESS | ISBN 978-1-910991-08-4 | IMPRESSION 1

www.ingramcontent.com/pod-product-compliance
Lightning Source LLC
Chambersburg PA
CBHW071325220526
45468CB00001B/499